Praying in serious illness

Nicholas Hutchinson, FSC

Matthew James Publishing Ltd

Also available by the same author

Praying Each Day of the Year – January to April
ISBN 978-1-898366-30-0

Praying Each Day of the Year – May to August
ISBN 978-1-898366-31-7

Praying Each Day of the Year – September to December
ISBN 978-1-898366-32-4

Lord, Teach us to Pray
ISBN 978-1-898366-65-2

Walk in My Presence – volume 1
ISBN 978-1-898366-60-7

Walk in My Presence – volume 2
ISBN 978-1-898366-76-8

Published by
Matthew James Publishing Ltd
19 Wellington Close
Chelmsford, Essex CM1 2EE
www.matthew-james.co.uk

Praying in serious illness
ISBN 978-1-898366-98-0

First published 2012

Printed by Biddles via MBC print consultancy

Dedicated
to the memory of
Brother Maximus Bangs, FSC
(1921-2008)
and
Brother Edmund Johnson, FSC
(1912-2009)
who put out their hands
and touched the face of God.

Contents

Foreword

Many people find it appropriate and heart-warming to start praying by reminding themselves that they are in the Presence of God (see Chapter 1) before moving to other themes of prayer.

Whilst it is not necessary to use words in prayer, it can be helpful to commit some words to paper and then return to them when the situation and feelings are similar again. It has been slowly over several years (and for my own use) that I prepared the texts in this book, given that M.E. and cancer are prominent in my life. Other people who are seriously ill – and their loved ones and carers – might find texts here that are of particular resonance. Indeed, I have been encouraged and heartened that individuals in difficult situations (and those accompanying them) have said that they have found draft copies of these texts to be especially helpful.

The texts of the 11 chapters are rich in scripture and can be taken in any order. You might want to dip into the book or take the prayers consecutively. The use of a pencil is to be encouraged in adding lines of your own to the prayers.

Most of the texts in the first half of the book I prepared a few years ago, and they are prayers for everyday use, whatever a person's journey. They can be well-used by people in good health, as well as serving as a good foundation for those in various stages of sickness. If I had had such a book at my fingertips throughout illness, it would have been well-used.

Item 50 is the pivotal passage of this 100-prayer book. That text explores the account of the illness and then the death of Lazarus, the special friend of Jesus (Jn 11), and the dialogue on that occasion is particularly touching.

May this book be of good service to you, whatever your pilgrim way, and may you be helped to write your own prayers so that, on returning to them, you will be enabled to read words again with which you will be well-able to identify.

May what is read in these pages be encouraging (Acts 15:31) and heartening (Philemon 1:7) to fellow-travellers and their loved ones, and may others be as touched in reading these prayers as I have been in writing them.

Charles Dickens wrote about his book, 'The Old Curiosity Shop':

> *"If I have put into my book*
> *anything which can fill the young mind*
> *with better thoughts of death,*
> *or soften the grief of older hearts;*
> *if I have written one word*
> *which can afford pleasure or consolation*
> *to old or young in time of trial,*
> *I shall consider it is something achieved*
> *– something which I shall be glad*
> *to look back upon*
> *in the afterlife."*

Brother Nicholas Hutchinson, FSC

De La Salle Brothers
7 Wokefield Way
St Helens
WA10 4QP
England

Nicholas@prayingeachday.org

November 2011

ONE
In the presence of God

1 YOU WALK BY MY SIDE

Today and always, Lord,
  you smile on me
  and embrace me with your love,
  walking by my side
  from the rising of the sun to its setting.
You have opened my eyes, good Lord,
  to the wonder of all that has been around me,
  and to the people
  who have been a part of my life each day.
Empower me with your Spirit
  and warm my heart again,
  and grant me to walk humbly
  with you, my God. Amen.

Nicholas Hutchinson

2 GOD'S HAND HOLDS ME FAST   *PSALM 138/139*

Lord, lover of life,
  you know the depths
  of my innermost self,
  and you understand me.
You protect me on every side,
  shielding me from all harm.

You formed me with care
  in my mother's womb,
  and you know all about me.
I thank you for the wonder of myself
  and I stand in awe
  at all that you have made
  and all that you do.
Guide me in your ways.

(Based on an extract of Psalm 139, which came to mind whilst having CT scans.)

On several occasions of having a CT scan, the themes and beautiful words of various translations of this psalm have readily come to mind: "you search me and you know me", "you probe me", "you discover what I am about", "you discern from afar"…

Nicholas Hutchinson

9

3 JESUS IN THE MIDST OF US

Betrayed and condemned, Lord,
    abandoned and tortured,
    your slow execution was between two thieves:
    'in the midst of them'.   *Jn 19:18*
We are reminded
    that you came to dwell among us,
    'in the midst' of people,   *Jn 1:14*
    and you have been called *'God-with-us'*.   *Mt 1:23*
As I pray, loving Lord,
    I ask you to remind me
    that you are here with me
    and are in the midst of your people
    who gather in your name.

Nicholas Hutchinson

4 WE NEED TO "LOOK" AND "REALLY SEE" SO AS TO ENCOUNTER JESUS IN OUR MIDST

Pieter Bruegel the Elder   *(c. 1525-1569)*
    in his *'Procession to Calvary'*
    depicts the Crucifixion happening
    somewhere in the middle of rushed daily life
    as many people mill about their business
    and their amusements.
The people know only too well
    that suffering abounds in their midst
    but, with so much frenetic activity,
    they are hardly likely to discover
    that the Son of God is in their midst.
The artist makes it difficult
    for us to see where Jesus is in the painting
    – and that is done deliberately, I think,
    partly reflecting our need to *'look'*,
    before we *'really see'*
    what is in our midst.

It is, perhaps, not a co-incidence,
that it is on sketching a cross through the painting,
dividing it into four equal rectangles,
that there, in the precise centre of the painting
(if we look carefully)
we can see the almost horizontal cross
being borne by Jesus.
Yes, right here in our midst
Jesus is to be found
if only we will look,
and if only our eyes are really open
for us to see, for us to perceive.
Indeed, in this painting it is the cross that we see
before we perceive Jesus himself,
perhaps pointing out to us
that if we see a cross being carried
in our midst today
it can lead us to see Jesus
as the one who is bearing
– or helping to bear – that burden….
Yes, almost lost in this painting,
and almost lost
in the human ordinariness of everyday life
is Jesus
– yet it is he who gives meaning
to the ordinariness of everyday life;
he is our meaning
and, in the busyness of our world,
he is – in the words of T.S.Eliot –   *Four Quartets*
"at the still-point of the turning world".   *'Burnt Norton'*

Nicholas Hutchinson

www.navigo.com/wm/paint/auth/bruegel/calvary.jpg
http://cgfa.sunsite.dk/bruegel1/p-brueg1-8.htm

5 TAKING UP OUR OWN CROSS

A cross
    (or a 'crucifix', if it portrays the body of Jesus)
    reminds me, Father,
    not only of much concerning
    the life, death and resurrection
    of Jesus, your Son and my Brother,   *Lk 9:23*
    but also that Jesus invites me
    to take up my own cross each day
    and follow him.

Years ago I tended to think
    that the 'carrying of a cross'
    often referred to a pious 'putting-up-with'
    minor irritating habits
    that each of us faces.
And here I am, Father,
    in a much clearer light,
    having encountered individuals
    carrying their own cross
    in very significant ways.
I reflect that I am
    alongside my brothers and sisters,
    as each of us carries our own cross,
    all contributing to something so much greater
    as we join, together and in association,
    and form the Body of Christ.

Nicholas Hutchinson

6 IT IS HERE AND IT IS TODAY THAT JESUS BRINGS SALVATION TO US

It is always **today** that you challenge us, Father.   *Deut 30:19*
You set before us
　a blessing or a curse:
　to choose life or death today,
　and the psalmist says:
　"O that today
　you would listen to God's voice."   *Ps 95:7*

At the start of the Gospel,
　is the Good News to each of us:
　'Today in the town of David   *Lk 2:11*
　a Saviour is born for you,'
　and at the start
　of the public ministry of Jesus,   *Lk 4:21*
　he reads from a scroll
　in the synagogue of his home-town of Nazareth.
There he concludes the prophecy from Isaiah, saying:
　"Today, here in your presence
　this text is being fulfilled."
And, later, to the diminutive Zacchaeus,
　high up in the tree,
　Jesus proclaims:
　"Hurry, Zacchaeus!   *Lk 19:5*
　because **I must stay with you today.**
　This day salvation has come to your house."
And in the prayer that Jesus taught us,
　the Lord says:
　*"Give us **this** day our daily bread"*   *Mt 6:11*
　and adds
　"Do not worry about tomorrow: *Mt 6:34*
　tomorrow will take care of itself.
　Each day has enough trouble of its own."
To the Good Thief beside him on the cross
　Jesus promises:
　"Today you will be with me in paradise."   *Lk 23:43*
Lead me, Lord, to live fully each day
　and recognise you in our midst.

Nicholas Hutchinson

13

7 YOUR PRESENCE IN OUR EVERYDAY LIVES

Brother Jesus,
  your presence is interwoven
  throughout each day of our lives.
As we journey with our companions,
  touch our hearts and open our eyes
  that we may recognise you
  walking beside us.
Lead us to live in such a way
  that we discover you
  in the quietness and in the spaces,
  as well as in the busyness
  of our lives each day.
Continue to call us your friends
  and accompany us
  to where we shall see our Father,
  face-to-face. Amen.

Nicholas Hutchinson

8 THE RICH YOUNG MAN   *– reflecting on Mark 1:17-22*

1. Lord Jesus,
     it must have been with great love
     that you touched the heart of the rich young man:
     "you looked steadily at him and loved him".

2. You reminded him of the commandments,
     and I like to think that he replied sincerely
     when he said that he had kept them all
     from his earliest days.

3. When I tend to place my trust
     in the good deeds and intentions of my earlier days,
     remind me that it is always *"today"*
     that you look steadily at me and show me your love,
     and that it is "today" that you call me to follow you.

4. However faithful he was
   in living the commandments,
   "he turned away sad",
   trusting in the wealth of his own efforts
   rather than in your freely-given grace.
   There is a temptation
   to consider my wealth for the next life
   to accrue from a credit of good works
   at the end of each day!
   Do remind me
   that, important as good works are,
   they are a response to your grace,
   freely offered to me.

5. May your look of love transform my heart,
   and enable me to follow you more closely,
   that I may discover you to be my greatest wealth.
   Challenge me each day;
   continue to look steadily at me,
   and empower me with your Spirit.

6. I like to think
   that you often remembered the young man
   in the months ahead,
   and continued to love him greatly,
   and that you prayed for him
   in the silence of your heart.
   Remember me, too,
   and strengthen me with the conviction
   that you often pray for me
   at the right hand of our Father.

Nicholas Hutchinson

9 THE CANTICLE OF CREATION *by St Francis of Assisi*

The saint usually associated above all others with an awareness of and sensitivity to the creatures and creation of God is St Francis of Assisi, and this beautiful prayer of his is called 'The Canticle of Creation':

1   O Most High, all-powerful, good Lord God,
     to you belong praise, glory,
     honour and all blessing.

2   Be praised, my Lord, for all your creation
     and especially for our Brother Sun,
     who brings us the day and the light;
     he is strong and shines magnificently.
     O Lord, we think of you when we look at him.

3   Be praised, my Lord, for Sister Moon,
     and for the stars
     which you have set shining and lovely
     in the heavens.

4   Be praised, my Lord,
     for our Brothers Wind and Air
     and every kind of weather
     by which you, Lord,
     uphold life in all your creatures.

5   Be praised, my Lord, for Sister Water,
     who is very useful to us,
     and humble and precious and pure.

6   Be praised, my Lord, for Brother Fire,
     through whom
     you give us light in the darkness:
     he is bright and lively and strong.

7   Be praised, my Lord,
    for Sister Earth, our Mother,
    who nourishes us and sustains us,
    bringing forth
    fruits and vegetables of many kinds
    and flowers of many colours.

8   Be praised, my Lord,
    for those who forgive for love of you;
    and for those
    who bear sickness and weakness
    in peace and patience
    – you will grant them a crown.

9   Be praised, my Lord, for our Sister Death,
    whom we must all face.

10 I praise and bless you, Lord,
    and I give thanks to you,
    and I will serve you in all humility.

TWO
Alone with only you, my God

10 WORTH MORE THAN HUNDREDS OF SPARROWS

On realising that the course of chemotherapy (given after an operation to remove the cancer) had not achieved the desired result, I wanted to write a prayer that would express confidence, faith and trust: words which I have used often since:

When I gaze at the heavens, Father,   *Ps 8*
   which your fingers have formed,
   I see the moon that you have set there
   and the stars that you call by name   *Ps 147:4*
   – yet my own name
   is written on the palm of your hands.   *Is 49:16*
I realise how small we are   *Ps 8*
   in the magnificence of your creation,
   yet you treasure each of us
   above all that you have made:
   making us only a little less than yourself,
   crowning us with so many good things.

In our world that you love so much, Father,   *Jn 3:16*
   I see the beauty of the flowers of the field   *Lk 12:27*
   and of the birds of the air,
   and I know that each of us
   is worth more than hundreds of sparrows.   *Lk 12:7*
Help me to appreciate, Father,
   that you love all that you have made,   *Wis 11:24*
   and enable me to experience deep within
   that I am precious to you   *Is 43:1*
   and am loved for who I am.
Show me how to proclaim
   in my life every day
   that each of us is your work of art   *Eph 2:10*
   and is made magnificently.   *Ps 139:14*

Nicholas Hutchinson

11 JESUS LOOKS STEADILY AT ME AND LOVES ME

May Jesus open my eyes, Father,   *Lk 24:31; Jn 9:32*
  that I may see
  that he looks steadily at me
  and loves me.   *Mk 10:17-22*
He kisses me tenderly   *Lk 15:20*
  and calls me his friend.   *Jn 15:15*

Let me experience deep within
  that you do heal the broken-hearted   *Ps 147:3*
  and you bind up all our wounds.
Then, Father, when life is difficult
  and problems crowd in,
  lead me to discover
  that there is no pit so deep
  that your love is not deeper still.
I rejoice
  that nothing can ever separate me
  from your love.   *Rom 8:39*
Amen.

12 LOOKING AT ME AND LOVING ME

Lord Jesus
  you treasure
  and hold a special place
  for each and every person,
  as though only that one individual exists.
I rejoice that you accept me as I am,
  in the reality of my life this day.
I rejoice, too, that though alone
  I need never feel lonely:
  I can grow in enjoying my own company
  and in appreciating, good Lord,
  that you are with me.
May I grow in the faith
  that you look steadily at me   *Mk 10:21*
  and love me tenderly. Amen.   *Lk 15:20*

Nicholas Hutchinson

13 WHAT 'HOME' CAN MEAN

In a programme (26/7/07) about the
footballer David Beckham, whose family homes
include locations in England and Los Angeles
and Madrid, Beckham told of a question he asked
one of his children. *"Which home do you like best?"*
he asked, and the child's delightful response was
to this effect: *"Wherever you and Mummy are:
that's our best home."*

14 "HIS HOMELIEST HOME"

St Julian of Norwich (1342-1420) reflects on
Jesus choosing to make his home in us, and
finding there that *"we are his homeliest home"*.

15 AN ICON

An icon is *'a window into heaven'*
and, for those who have eyes to see,
an icon also reflects your presence here, Lord,
in our lives and in our circumstances this day.

Icons are said to be 'written' rather than painted
and, in their preparation,
icon-writers spend much time in prayer and fasting,
placing themselves in your hands, Lord,
knowing that, in doing so,
their hands and skills will be 'guided'
to produce an icon that will convey
something of your presence, Lord.

And so it is that the 'writing' of an icon
is the writing of a Word of God,
conveying much to us;
and so we can pray:
"Speak, Lord, your servant is listening."   *1 Sam 3:10*

Nicholas Hutchinson, FSC

www.biblik.com/images/icone_christ_jean_clemence.jpg

This icon is of John leaning against Jesus at the Last Supper, and the accompanying words in French, are: 'I will bind you to myself in tenderness and love': Hos 2:19/21.

This icon
shows St John close to you at the Last Supper,
and corresponds with what John writes:
that 'we have heard the Word who is life: *1 Jn 1:1*
we have seen him with our own eyes
and have touched him with our hands'.
As I am seriously ill,
I ask that I may grow as close to you
as John is portrayed to be,
because I long to meet you face-to-face.

Nicholas Hutchinson

16 INVITING THE LORD TO MAKE HIS HOME IN ME

I recall, Lord Jesus,
  that you told your disciples
  to go into their *"inner room"* to pray.   *Mt 6:6*
And so here I am, Lord,
  in **my** "inner room",
  my own special place.
Not only is it somewhere
  where I feel comfortable
  and can readily be myself,
  but it serves as a reminder
  to come to you in a genuine way,
  just as I am,
  with no pretence or insincerity
  that only build up walls of separation
  – whether with other people,
  or with you.
Whenever I am anxious
  or afraid, Lord,   *Mt 6:34, Jn 14:1*
  or am not really myself,
  and *"the doors of my room*
  are closed",   *Jn 20:19*
  do come through those doors
  and be with me
  and bring me your peace.
Then, with courage
  and with the strength of your Spirit,
  those doors, too, will be opened.

You told a friend to ask
"Where is the room
in which I can eat the Passover
with my disciples?"   *Lk 22:11*
My answer, Lord, is **here**:
  because I am keen
  that there always be room
  in my life for you.   *Lk 2:7*
I open my door
  as I hear you
  calling me and knocking   *Rev 3:20*
  and I invite you to come in,
  knowing that you are **ready**
  to join me, side by side.
As with any other guest in my home, Lord,
  I welcome you warmly,
  and I hear you say:
  "Make your home in me
  as I make mine in you." Amen.   *Jn 15:4*

Nicholas Hutchinson

23

17 THAT YOU HAVE MADE YOUR HOME IN ME, LORD

1. Jesus said: *Mt 11:28*
   Come to me, all you who have heavy burdens,   *Jn 14:27*
   and I will give you rest.
   Peace is what I leave with you
   – my own peace.
   Do not be worried or upset;
   do not be afraid.
   I rejoice, Lord,
   that you have made your home in me
   and call me your friend.

2. Jesus said: *Mt 9:29*
   Be healed;   *Jn 5:8*
   get up and walk;   *Jn 11:44*
   unbind him;   *Mk 2:5*
   your sins are forgiven;   *Mk 1:41*
   be clean;   *Mk 5:34*
   go in peace and be healed of your trouble.
   I rejoice, Lord,
   that you have made your home in me
   and call me your friend.

3. Jesus said: *Jn 15:15*
   I do not call you servants;   *Jn 13:34*
   I call you friends.   *Mt 18:20*
   As I have loved you,
   so you must love one another.
   When two or three come together in my name,
   I will be there with you.
   I rejoice, Lord,
   that you have made your home in me
   and call me your friend.

4. Jesus said: *Jn 6:35*
   Those who come to me   *Jn 4:14*
   will never be hungry or thirsty again.   *Jn 7:38*
   The life-giving water that I will give   *Jn 14:16*
   is the Holy Spirit.
   I will ask the Father,
   and he will give you the Holy Spirit:
   the 'Helper'.
   I rejoice, Lord,
   that you have made your home in me
   and call me your friend.

5. Jesus said: *Jn 15:5*
   I am the vine and you are the branches.   *Jn 10:10*
   Those who remain in me, and I in them,
   will bear much fruit.
   I have come that you may have life,
   life in all its fullness.
   I rejoice, Lord,
   that you have made your home in me
   and call me your friend.

6. Jesus said: *Jn 11:25*
   Those who believe in me will live,   *Jn 14:1-16*
   even though they die.
   I will prepare a place for you
   where I am going.
   I am the way, the truth, and the life;
   I am the Resurrection and the life.
   I rejoice, Lord,
   that you have made your home in me
   and call me your friend.

Nicholas Hutchinson

18 AT HOME WITH GOD

The Lord says
that he is at home in my house   *Numbers 12:7*
and he speaks with me
face-to-face.

19 CHILD/PARENT RELATIONSHIPS

God our Father,
   many rejoice that you call them your daughter.
I happen to rejoice that you call me your son,
   and I much appreciate
   that you invite me to live
   in the closeness of that father-son relationship.
Over years of teaching teenagers
   I can think of many parents I have met,
   and if I call to mind
   what I thought was 'best'
   in the many fathers and mothers I met,
   and if I think, too,
   of the insights I gained into the best of relationships
   of son-and-father
   within my own extended family,
   then I rejoice in all that has been very good
   in what I have seen.
And I go on to acknowledge, Father,
   that what you offer us, and what you invite us to
   exceeds the very best
   in all the relationships
   I have encountered over the years.

It is that word 'encounter'
  that I often return to in my prayer,
  appreciating the many ways
  in which I have, indeed, encountered you in the past
  whenever my side of the relationship
  has grown less warm, less 'full of life',
  and you are already looking out for me,   *Lk 15:20*
  running to greet me,
  clasping me in your arms.
And then many images come to mind
  – of the return of the prodigal son, of course,
  and of wonderful examples
  of human warmth between people.
Again, it is always the case
  that **you, Lord, exceed the very best**
  of what I have experienced or imagined.

Nicholas Hutchinson, FSC

20 SCRIPTURE REFLECTION ON BEING GOD'S FRIEND

A particular icon is often associated with Taizé,
the ecumenical international prayer centre in France,
and it portrays the right hand of Jesus resting
on the shoulder of his friend.
It is a very poignant and gentle image.

It is an Egyptian 6th/7th Century Coptic icon
of Jesus, with his hand on the shoulder of Saint Menas,
a former soldier who became a monk, who was martyred
in 296. The icon is displayed in The Louvre in Paris.
It is good to grow more aware of being in the presence
of God. That reflects, of course, awareness of the relationship
of friendship to which we are called (Jn 15:15).

http://en.wikipedia.org/wiki/Image:Menas.jpg
www.stespritnyc.org/parish-life-taize.html
and is often called 'The Icon of Friendship'.

21 LISTENING TO THE SCRIPTURES UNFOLD ON OUR JOURNEY

cf Luke 24

Loving Lord,
 it is good to be here beside you
 and listen to the Scriptures unfold
 as you speak.
The healing word that you bring
 begins with the calling of my name,
 and I hear you say
 that you are my Brother and my Friend.
I rejoice that I am dear to you,
 and that you want to listen
 to what I would like to say.
And so I thank you
 that my prayer can be
 a close sharing between friends.

You go beyond words,
 and your hand upon my shoulder
 enfolds me in your love
 and encourages and comforts me.
I pray that nothing but your love
 will ever overwhelm me,
 so that I may grow
 as the extraordinary person
 you call me to be.

I pray, too, for other pilgrims,
 that we may strengthen one another
 on our common journey.
Teach me, my Brother and Friend,
 to remain faithful.
And when I arrive home,
 you will be there beside me still
 and, together, we will know
 the welcoming embrace of our Father.

Nicholas Hutchinson

THREE
Links in a chain
(a sense of belonging)

22 REMEMBERING THOSE WHO HAVE DIED

Karl Rahner, SJ
'Encounters with Silence', Chapter 7
(Burns & Oates 1975), adapted

I should like to remember my dead before you,
O Lord: all those who were once part of me
and who have now left me.... When I look back
in this way, I see my life as a long highway
filled by a column of marching people. Every
moment someone breaks out of the line and
goes off silently, without a word or wave
of farewell, to be swiftly enwrapped in the
darkness of the night, stretching out on both
sides of the road....

One day I myself will have to break off from
the line of march, and leave without a word of
farewell, never more to return.

I think of those who were with me at the very
start of my journey to You, my God: the dear
ones who were, and still are, close to my
heart. There are no substitutes for my loved
ones; there are no others who can fill the
vacancy when one of those whom I have really
loved, suddenly and unexpectedly departs
and is with me no more. In true love no one
can replace another, for true love loves the
other person in that depth where they are
uniquely and irreplaceably themselves.

23 OUR HERITAGE OF FAITH

This prayer reflects on so many people who have played their part in passing on to us the rich heritage of faith:

God our Father,
    if I could trace back
    through the last two thousand years,
    marking out routes
    from Jesus himself
    and then through people
    whose faith has touched others
    and so reached me,
    I would be astounded
    by the individuals I would encounter.
I give thanks, Father,
    for all those people
    who have inspired others
    and played their part
    in passing on
    to generation after generation
    the living heritage of their faith.

As I reflect these days
    on the time lying ahead of me,
    I give thanks especially
    for all relatives and friends and colleagues
    who have gone before us in your love,
    marked with the sign of faith.
We remember
    how they have touched our lives
    and the lives of others
    and have shared the Good News of your love.
I am grateful, Father,
    that the lives and deaths of many people
    have had good influence on us.

We give thanks
  for those who lived their faith
  through hardship and persecution
  hundreds of years ago.
Other kinds of persecution can be concealed
  behind a veneer of respectability,
  and we give thanks, too,
  for those who have lived faithfully in our own days:
  those who have faced different kinds
  of hatred and destruction
  in being belittled, diminished and discouraged
  especially when treated in those ways
  by others who profess to proclaim the Gospel.

Touch the hearts of all of us, Father,
  that we may see ourselves and others
  as you see us,
  and so give thanks for what is good.
Root out any evil that masquerades as goodness.

Through good times and bad, Father,
  may we grow in your faith and love.
Amen.

Nicholas Hutchinson, FSC

Praying Each Day of the Year,
(Matthew James Publishers)
Volume 2, Text for 1 August

24   A LINK IN A CHAIN

Blessed John Henry Newman
From 'Meditations on Christian Doctrine'

1. Let us put ourselves into his hands,
   and not be startled
   though he leads us by a strange way.
   Let us be sure he will lead us right,
   that he will lead us to that which is,
   not indeed what we think best,
   not what is best for another,
   but what is best for us.
   We are all created for his glory
   – we are created to do his will.

2. I am created to do something or to be something
   for which no-one else is created;
   I have a place in God's counsels, in God's world,
   which no-one else has,
   whether I be rich or poor,
   despised or esteemed by others:
   God knows me and calls me by name.

3. God has created me
   to do him some definite service.
   He has committed some work to me
   which he has not committed to another.
   I have my mission
   – I may never know it in this life,
   but I shall be told it in the next.
   Somehow I am necessary for his purposes;
   I have a great part in his work.

4. I am a link in a chain,
   a bond of connection between persons.
   He has not created me for nothing.
   I shall do good, I shall do his work.

5. I shall be an angel of peace,
   a preacher of truth in my own place,
   while not intending it,
   if I do but keep his commandments,
   and serve him in my calling.
   Therefore I will trust him.

6. Whatever, wherever I am,
   I can never be thrown away.
   If I am in sickness, my sickness may serve him;
   if I am in perplexity, my perplexity may serve him;
   if I am in sorrow, my sorrow may serve him.
   My sickness or perplexity or sorrow
   may be necessary causes of some great end
   which is quite beyond us.
   He does nothing in vain;
   he may prolong my life, he may shorten it;
   he knows what he is about.

6. Lord, I give myself to you;
   I trust you wholly.
   You are wiser than I
   – more loving to me than I am to myself.
   Fulfil your great purposes in me,
   whatever they may be.
   Work in and through me.
   I am born to serve you, to be yours.

FOUR
Change of heart; forgiveness

25 GENEROSITY OF THE FATHER'S LOVE

Loving Father,
    you tell us in the Bible
    that whatever wrongs we have done
    you tread down our faults
    and cast our sins
    to the bottom of the sea.   *Mic 7:19*

We know that there is no need
    to keep thinking
    about what we have done in the past,   *Is 43:18*
    because you pardon
    the wrongs we have done,
    and you delight in showing mercy.   *Mic 7:18*

Lord, you love
    all that you have made,   *Wis 11:24*
    and it is your very nature
    to love and forgive.
You bind up all our wounds   *Ps 147:3*
    and you renew us by your love.   *Zeph 3:17*

Lead each of us every day
    to look upon ourselves and one another
    in the same gracious way
    that you smile and look upon us.
We give thanks that your love and forgiveness,
    your mercy and compassion,
    all exceed our own generosity.

Remind us each day, Father,
    that nothing can ever separate us
    from your love   *Rom 8:31-39*
    as we see it in Jesus, your Son.
Amen.

Nicholas Hutchinson

26 PENITENTIAL PRAYER

(The Lost Son – 'The Prodigal Son')

*This prayer is particularly poignant when used alongside Rembrandt's painting,
'The Return of the Prodigal Son' – websites of which are given below, after the
text of the prayer. The parable itself (one of three 'lost' parables in Luke 15) has
been described as "the gospel within the gospel", so well does it portray the
message of Jesus.*

God our Father,
    so much around me and within me
    summons me to grow in wonder
    at all that you have made,
    and to be thankful
    for all the blessings you bring
    each day of my life.

I know of the life and love and dignity
    to which you call me,
    and I am aware, too,
    that I distort that vision
    whenever I choose to live
    according to other attractions.

Give me that special grace of yours, Father,
    that opens my heart
    to accept that you love me tenderly.
Lead me to rejoice
    that you run to greet me
    and embrace me with joy,
that you cast behind your back
    the wrong that I have done,
that no pit is so deep
    that your love is not deeper still.

continues...

And so, Father, I acknowledge my sinfulness
and I place my trust
in your mercy and compassion.
Purify me and cleanse me;
release me from whatever binds me,
and blot out all my guilt.
Anoint my wounds with your life-giving Spirit
and then, healed and made whole,
I will express my thanks to you
through the way I will seek to live each day.

Empower me with your Spirit
so that I may grow in faithfulness
as the person you call me to be. Amen.

Nicholas Hutchinson

Webpages of Rembrandt's 'The Return of the Prodigal Son':

www.ibiblio.org/wm/paint/auth/rembrandt/1660/return-prodigal-son.jpg
www.artofeurope.com/rembrandt/rem14.htm
www.artchive.com/artchive/R/rembrandt/prodigal_son.jpg.html
www.wga.hu/frames-e.html?/html/r/rembran/painting/biblic3/prodig2.html

27 JESUS TRANSFORMED SUFFERING WITH HIS PRESENCE

Lord Jesus,
in coming among us
you did not seek to explain suffering
but you filled it with your presence
and changed people's lives.
Lead us to grow more aware of your presence
in all that is ordinary
– today and each day of our lives. Amen.

Nicholas Hutchinson

28 CHRIST'S LOVE IS ALWAYS GREATER...

*Corrie Ten Boom was a Dutch Christian
holocaust survivor, who helped many
Jews escape. The film 'The Hiding Place'
concerns the lives of her family.*

**"There is no pit so deep
that Christ's love
is not deeper still."**

29 BREAKING THE CYCLE OF EVIL

God our Father,
   I know that to forgive someone
   can be far from being an easy option,
   and I know that forgiveness
   isn't somehow pretending
   that something wrong hasn't happened.
For what I have done wrong, Father,
   forgive me in the same way
   that I am generous and gracious in forgiving
   – or truly hoping to forgive –
   those who have done wrong to me.
Empower me to break the cycle
   of any hatred, resentment or bitterness,
   always resisting evil
   and conquering it with goodness. Amen.

Nicholas Hutchinson

FIVE
Offering, transforming

30 A DAILY OFFERING

Lord Jesus,
  you told your friends
  not to worry about the future.
You showed them
  how to have the attitude
  of simple trust
  that young children have,
  so that they could place themselves
  into the caring hands of our Father.
And so I ask for the power of your Spirit
  that I may remain positive
  throughout all that happens
  each day of my life,
  knowing that nothing
  can ever separate me
  from your love.
I know that your touch
  can change people and situations,
  and so I ask you
  to join me in offering to our Father
  not only the good things of this day,
  but also any suffering and sacrifices
  that I want to offer
  cheerfully and lovingly,
  and in a quiet and hidden way.
And so may any difficulties
  and frustration and pain of this day
  be transformed in your presence
  for the benefit of other people.
Amen.

Nicholas Hutchinson

31 EMPTY HANDS

With your hands, Lord Jesus,
  you heal and forgive,
  and you transform inadequacies –
  such as the loaves and fish
  – into an abundance.

Whenever our hands are tightened
  into fists of anger, frustration or anxiety,
  free us, Lord,
  that we may open our hands
  and offer them to you.
Then, as we come to you and our Father
  with empty hands,
  remove from us
  whatever holds us back and restricts us.
Make us whole within.

Nicholas Hutchinson

32 STRENGTHENED FOR THE FUTURE

God our Father,
  in good times
  may I live in such a way
  that I will be strengthened
  for the difficult times
  that all of us face in our lives.
Lead me now
  to make positive choices
  to value friendship and loyalty,
  and develop attitudes and values,
  treasuring all that is lasting and important.
Throughout difficult times
  may I build on
  the positive choices of my past,
looking outward in the service of others
  and avoiding self-pity.
May I grow in the faith
  that, whatever my circumstances,
I need have no regrets.

Nicholas Hutchinson

33 CHALLENGES AND CHOICES

John Powell, SJ in this text, outlines questions which challenge us as to the choices we make, upon which our way of living is then built:

It is obvious to me that each new day
– along with all the persons and events
of that day –
does in fact question us,
if we will submit to the test.
The needy, unattractive person
asks me how much I can love.
The death of a dear one
asks me what I really believe about death,
and how profitably I can confront
loss and loneliness.
A beautiful day and a beautiful person
ask me how capable I am of enjoyment.
Solitude asks me if I really like myself
and enjoy my own company.
A good joke asks me if I have a sense of humour.
A very different type of person
from a background very dissimilar to my own,
asks me if I am capable
of empathy and understanding.
Success and failure
ask me to define my ideas of success and failure.
Suffering asks me
if I really believe I can grow through adversity.
Negative criticism directed to me
asks me about
my sensitivities and self confidence.
The devotion and commitment of another to me,
asks me if I will let myself be loved.

*John Powell: 'Fully Human, Fully Alive',
pg 92 (Tabor Publishing, California)*

34 PRAYER OF SILENCE AND OF WORDS, OF OFFERING AND OF INTERCESSION

Often, Lord Jesus, I've said to you
   that I offer my circumstances,
   asking that they be transformed
   into something good for others.

Frequently the way I pray
   is to raise my open hand
   or trace a cross on myself.
They are simple ways of praying,
   especially useful
   when it's difficult to find words of offering.
And silent suffering, of course,
   can be prayer in itself.

For my own sake, though,
   I find it useful at times
   to put into words
   what I feel I need to offer
   to be transformed on your cross.

And so, Lord,
   whilst I offer you in general
   the pain and the difficulties,
   I offer
   what I'm particularly conscious of at present:
   the weariness and frustration....

In making this prayer of offering
   I also wish to remember in your presence
   particular people and intentions....

Nicholas Hutchinson

35 NOTHING IS TOO DEEP THAT YOUR LOVE CANNOT REACH IT

God, Father of us all,
    you who call me by name: *Is 43:1*
    you are my hiding-place,
    my shelter,   *Ps 32:1*
    amidst life's difficulties.
Remind me
    that there is no pit, no hole, so deep
    that your love
    is not deeper still.
Lead me to give thanks
    in all my circumstances,   *1 Thess 5:18*
    and show me how to transform
    whatever suffering or difficulties
    I may experience,
    into something that will benefit others
    and will set me free.
I make this prayer,
    knowing that you
    lavish your love upon us   *1 Jn 3:1*
    and you set
    the down-trodden free.   *Is 61:1; Lk 4:18*
Amen.

Nicholas Hutchinson

36 THE SACRAMENT OF THE PRESENT MOMENT

God our Father, it is in you
  that we live and move
  and have our being.   *Acts 17:28*
Inspire us to live in such a way
  that our choices each day
  may lead us to live faithfully the present moment
  and transform the ordinariness of daily life
  into something extraordinary.
Bless us this day and always. Amen.

Nicholas Hutchinson

37 TRANSFORM ILLNESS

Pope John Paul II
for the World Day of the Sick, 11.2.94

"Dear people who are ill, sustained by faith…
  take the opportunity
  opened up by Christ
  to transform your situation
  into an expression of grace and love.
Then your pain, too, will become salvific
  and contribute to completing
  the suffering of Christ
  for the benefit of his Body,
  which is the Church…   *(c.f. Col 1:24)*
Happy is the person
  who succeeds in making God's light shine
  in the poverty of a suffering or diminished life."

SIX
Thanks for many blessings

38 SAYING 'THANK YOU'

Meister Eckhart, the Dominican mystic, wrote:

"If the only prayer
you say in your whole life
is *'Thank you'*,
that would suffice."

39 THE GREATEST SAINTS ARE THOSE WHO EXPRESS THANKS TO GOD

William Law (1686-1761)
'A Serious Call to a Devout and Holy Life'

Would you know
    who is the greatest saint in the world?
It is not he who prays most or fasts most;
    it is not he who gives most alms
    or is most eminent
    for temperance, chastity or justice;
    but it is he
    who is always thankful to God,
    who wills everything that God wills,
    who receives everything that God wills,
    who receives everything
    as an instance of God's goodness,
    and has a heart
    always ready to praise God for it...

40 FOCUS ON BLESSINGS

Charles Dickens shares this valuable insight:

"Reflect upon your present blessings,
of which everyone has plenty,
and not on your present misfortunes,
of which all have some".

(Sketches by Boz, Chapter 2)

41 BEING BLESSINGS FOR OTHERS

Father, I give thanks,
   for all who have shown me much love and care
   in so many different ways.
I give thanks
   for many who have touched my heart
   over the years,
   in whose faces, words and actions
   your love and compassion, too, Father,
   have been reflected.

I give thanks
   for all who have looked for the best in me
   and for all
   whose love and kindness
   and care and encouragement
   have been tangible.
They have been a great blessing for me.

Certainly there are times
   when a gesture of kindness from an individual
   becomes even more than that:
   when, in your Providence,
   such goodness also serves
   as a very special gesture of your love and concern.
And so, with the eyes of faith, good Lord,
   some occurrences I can call **"God's kisses"**:
   gestures of love and compassion,
   of presence and understanding,
   of promise and assurance
   – all given when there is a special need.

When days are rough
   I might forget my blessings for a while
   and then you send another of your 'kisses',
   leading me to see you and others and myself
   in a different light.

I thank you, too, good Lord,
   for those people
   who consider me to be a blessing for them,
   and I rejoice in the abundance
   of your graces and blessings, Father,
   being the most abundant
   in the person of Jesus, your Son and our Brother,
   through whom I now offer this and all my prayers.
   Amen.

Nicholas Hutchinson

42 THANKFUL FOR OTHERS

So warmly, so richly
  have you blessed each of us,
  and I have so much to be grateful for   *cf Eph 5:20*
  and so much to pray for   *cf Phil 4:6*
  as I think of those
  who are particularly close to me now.
I have many people in mind, Father,
  – those who are alive
  and also those who have gone ahead of me
  into the fullness of salvation,
  where all of us hope to share in your glory.

When my time of death comes, Father,
  I ask that you will admit me
  into the fullness of your presence.
I am full of confidence in asking you, Father,
  about wanting to make my home with you   *2 Cor 5:9*
  and be surrounded there by many loved ones.

I know that the life and death of each of us
  has its influence to bear on others.   *cf Rom 14:7-12*
  and as I pray to you now, Father,
  I am grateful in particular
  for those who have been
  of support and encouragement in these times.
I ask, Father, that you comfort them
  with the same consolation
  that you have given to me.   *2 Cor 1:4*

In the time remaining to me, Father,
  I rejoice that you are in our midst   *Zeph 3:14*
  and that you renew me by your love.
Within, I feel renewed day by day,   *2 Cor 4:16*
  and I ask especially
  that you keep me grateful
  for so many blessings,   *Eph 1:3*
  and keep me ever-cheerful. Amen.

Nicholas Hutchinson

SEVEN
"Lord, the one you love is ill"

43   GOING FOR TESTS

Lord Jesus,
   I am going for tests,
   and I would rather know
   what is amiss at this time
   than have banks of tests in the future.

My prayer is that the results
   reflect the reality
   – whatever that might be –
   of my circumstances.

Then I hope
   to have fuller knowledge and understanding,
   and so be the more likely
   to be better at moving on
   to another phase, another stage, of my life.

Lead me to appreciate and value
   the many ways
   in which I have been blessed
   over the years.

Nicholas Hutchinson

44 ABOUT TO RECEIVE TEST RESULTS

Lord, may the results of recent tests
  reflect the reality
  and point the way forward
  as to what is amiss with me.

Guide the skills and expertise
  of the medical staff I encounter,
  and may the diagnosis
  be specific.

May all who are ill
  experience medical people
  who are skilled in specialities
  and are richly endowed
  with care and compassion.

Nicholas Hutchinson

45 TRANSFUSION

O my Lord and God,
the journey is too great for me
unless you feed me
with bread from heaven and wine of life,
unless you share with me
your own life.

I need, O Father,
a transfusion of the spiritual blood
of your Risen Son,
flowing through the arteries of my spirit.
May his strength
be my strength,
his love be my love
and his will my will,
victorious over sin, ill-will,
self-centredness and death.
O Lord, my God,
O Christ, your Son.

George Appleton ('One Man's Prayers' – SPCK)

46 DESCRIBING PAIN

Sometimes, Lord Jesus, I find it difficult
  to describe or quantify pain:
  "Is it sharp?" I am asked;
  "What number would you use to describe the pain
  on a 1-to-10 scale?"
It can be problematic because, of course,
  even toothache
  can become all-encompassing.

At times I feel pain
  and then, after a while,
  it is good
  that I often become somewhat 'distanced'
  from the pain,
  so that its effects are dulled.
It can be tricky, therefore,
  to describe just what the pain is like.
And yet I know that the medical people
  want some personalised information
  to help them assess what is going on.

I ask you to keep me cheerful, Lord,
  and to experience in my heart
  the great tenderness and compassion
  you have for each of us.

I repeat to you
  what friends said to you about your friend Lazarus,
  "Lord, the one you love is ill".

Nicholas Hutchinson

51

47 'DIFFICULT' RESULTS

Father,
  the results of recent tests
  have come in,
  and they reflect demanding circumstances.
Help me to continue to grow
  so that, with your grace,
  I can live as fully as possible
  within the changed parameters
  of my life.

Remind me that you invite me
  to place myself into your hands.
Remind me
  that it is not so much a matter
  of years in my life
  as of life in my years.

Remind me, too,
  that you call me still to have a part to play
  in sharing the Good News with others
  – especially as I remember
  the words of St Francis,
  who said to his followers
  "Preach the Gospel; if necessary, use words".

Nicholas Hutchinson

48 FOR THOSE WHO NEVER GET WELL

Look in kindness, Father,
  on those who suffer
  from constant sickness or weakness,
  and on those who never get well.
Give hope to the frustrated
  and to those who see no progress.
Give them the courage to share with Jesus
  in carrying their cross
  for the salvation of the world.
May their weaknesses become your opportunities,
  and help them always to praise you.

Nicholas Hutchinson, FSC

49 IN SERIOUS ILLNESS I HAVE NOT NEEDED TO SAY "WHY ME?"

Over the last 30 years or so,
   the living faith of some people I have encountered
   or have lived with
   has been a very great example to me
   and, amidst serious illness,
   I have never, for example, had occasion to say:
   "Why me?"
Yes, I grow frustrated at times
   when the going is very rough,
   and I do most certainly
   speak my mind to you, Father,
   but I am immensely grateful
   to remain at peace,
   continuing to choose what is 'of life',
   accepting and embracing each day.
I am so very glad, Father,
   that an attitude of *"Why me?"*
   just would not 'fit'
   with how I have always tried to live my life,
   with how I have encouraged
   young people to develop,
   with how I believe you and I get on together
   and with what I have read
   and have taken to heart from the scriptures.

Nicholas Hutchinson

50 MARTHA AND MARY
– the SICKNESS and RAISING from the DEAD of LAZARUS cf John 11

It is always very touching to read the account
  of the sickness of Lazarus.
It is abundantly clear
  that here were four very close friends:
  the blood family that was Lazarus
  and his sisters, Martha and Mary,
  and their close friend, evidently,
  was Jesus, the wandering preacher.
Martha and Mary
  were so concerned about their brother,
  that they sent this message to Jesus:
  "Lord, the one you love is ill."   *Jn 11:3*
What touching words
  to have been spoken by the sisters!
What poignant words
  to have been passed on by the messenger!
What challenging words for Jesus to hear,
  knowing that those words implied so much
  and conveyed trust and faith in him!

We are not told of any request
  that Jesus should rush there,
  but it is very evident
  that the sisters were informing Jesus
  of **serious** illness.
Yet they were also hoping
  – based on
  their mutual deep friendship and great love
  (and also believing in who Jesus was) –
  that Jesus would, indeed,
  do something for them all.
Martha and Mary presumed
  that, as he had cured many other people,
  now it would be the turn
  for something to happen
  to benefit their brother, Lazarus.

Yet, on receiving the message, Jesus said:

*"This sickness
will end not in death* Jn 11:4
*but in God's glory,
and through it
the Son of God will be glorified."*
That is a very powerful statement
   but was of no immediate help to any of them!

And it is followed by another such statement:
   *'Jesus loved Martha and her sister
   and Lazarus.'*   Jn 11:5
Yet, as we read, *Jesus did nothing
   for two more days.*
Only then did he say to his disciples,
   "Let us go to Judea."   Jn 11:7

Amongst so many very touching phrases is this,
   when Martha spoke to Jesus,
   still some distance away from their house:
   *"If you had been here,
   my brother would not have died,"*   Jn 11:21
   and the very same words
   were spoken by Mary
   on arrival at the house,   Jn 11:32
   reflecting their unity
   in love and friendship and faith.
This serves as a reminder to me
   that if Jesus is present
   – or, rather, if I am attuned to his presence –
   then LIFE will be there for me, too.

And so, for me, it is very poignant
   when looking at an icon of the Lord,
   gazing on that representation
   as a help in prayer.

*"Yes, Lord Jesus,
   I join Martha in proclaiming
   that you are the Christ, the Son of God,
   the One who was to come
   into our world.
Today, as every day,
   I am sure* continues...

that some of my friends in their prayer
will be remembering me.
They will be stating
that I am your friend, good Lord.
They will be repeating back to you
those gentle words
as, kindly,
they name me in prayer before you:

'Lord,

– _____ –

the one you love
is sick.'

They will remember, too, Lord,
that the gospel-writer makes note
that it was **'in great distress**   *Jn 11:33*
and with a sigh
that came straight from the heart
that you asked
where the body of Lazarus
had been put'.
Some of my friends will remind you, Lord,
of those two words that convey much
in the shortest sentence in the Bible.
And the two words in the Gospel text, Lord,
that conveyed much
about your love for Lazarus, were:
'Jesus wept'.   *Jn 11:36*
And so it was with good reason, Lord,
that people commented:
'See how much he loved him!' "

And I rejoice now
at how much you love **me,**
and I thank you.
I rejoice, too, that I have many friends
who are so very good and sincere.
I rejoice that they love me greatly,
and I rejoice that they can see
how much you love me, too."

Nicholas Hutchinson

51 COMPASSION AT THE HEART OF OUR PRAYER:

Letting down through the roof one who is ill

(reflecting on the Gospel passage of the man let down through the roof by his friends – Lk 5:17-26)

Loving Lord Jesus,
   we read in the Gospels
   that you spoke individually
   to many people,
   changing their lives
   as you showed them recognition and acceptance
   and as you brought them healing and wholeness.

We read, too,
   of how some people were such good friends
   of a man who was weak and paralysed,
   that they carried him on his stretcher:
   making their way through the crowds,
   carrying him on to the roof,
   and gently lowering him down,
   so that he could be right in front of you.
They must have been such good friends to him,
   and others could see
   the tenderness of their love and care
   as well as
   their extraordinary faith and trust in you, Lord,
   in bringing him into your presence.
And isn't it the very same
   that we are doing today, Lord
   – those of us who love and care for _____ –
   as we bring him, carry him,
   in the strength of our love
   into the warmth and light of your presence:
   knowing that you, too,
   are very fond of him?

continues...

We can all but hear you
    calling _____ by his name   *Is 43:1*
    as you are also calling him your friend,   *Jn 15:15*
    and we know that your love never fails.   *1 Cor 13:8*
Lord,
    _____ – "the one you love – is ill",   *Jn 11:3*
    and those of us who join you
    in loving him and caring for him
    ask you to lay your hands on him   *Lk 4:40; Mk 5:23*
    and transform his life once again,
    bringing him the fullness
    of your healing and your life. Amen.   *Jn 11:10*

Nicholas Hutchinson

52 HAVING AN OPERATION

Lord, I hate the very thought
    of having an operation
    – perhaps most of all because during that time
    I will lose control of my life.

Guide the hands of the doctors and nurses
    and help me to be relaxed,
    at ease and at peace.

Remind me that even in the operating theatre
    there can be something about me
    which can help to touch the hearts of others.

53 TO BE FREE FROM PAIN AND ANXIETY AND CONTINUE BEING POSITIVE IN SPIRIT

At this time, Father,
  I join others who are seriously ill
  in praying for ourselves and for our loved ones,
  and I recall words of Jesus to his close friends:
"Until now
  you have not asked for anything in my name.
Ask and you will receive,
  and so your joy will be complete."

Jn 16:24

Essentially, Father,
  in terms of physical, psychological ·
  and spiritual well-being
  I pray that I may be free of pain,
  and also be free from anything
  that might worry or trouble me,
  that might give rise to anxiety.

Jn 14:1; Ps 37:8;
cf Is 41:10

I remember years ago
  hesitating about a general anaesthetic
  before an operation
  – but the concern really, I think,
  was about 'not being in control of myself'.
As time moves on,
  and symptoms
  and especially some side-effects
  play more of a dominant part,
  I suppose it is all part of the greater 'letting go'.
Not feeling 'in charge' of what is happening to me
  is not a good feeling to have,
  and it's not because of pride or stubbornness,
  it's more a matter, Father,
  of knowing that some things will be quite beyond me.
I don't like the idea, at all,
  of being 'fragile' or disorientated in my mind,
  or of medicines making me hallucinate,
  of feeling 'delicate' or 'fuddled' in my mind.

continues...

Having had various unpleasant effects
　　from some morphine-based medication,
　　I need to add, Father,
　　my great need
　　to be free from any medication
　　that 'plays around with my head'!

Considering the flowers of the field   *Mt 6:25-34*
　　and the birds of the air,
　　I am very thankful that I continue to have
　　much joy in my heart,   *cf Rom 5:11*
　　much life and vitality
　　and enthusiasm in my spirit,
　　and I do seek to laugh
　　amidst my circumstances,
　　because having Christian hope   *Rom 12:12*
　　does make me cheerful.
The biblical Book of Proverbs reminds us
　　that *'a kindly word makes us glad,*   *Prov 12:25*
　　and worry makes a person's heart heavy'.
I continue to trust, Father,
　　in your loving care   *cf Ps 131*
　　because you have never let me down.

54   FEELING DIMINISHED IN ILLNESS

This prayer – written a couple of years after the commencement of the debilitating illness, Chronic Fatigue Syndrome (M.E.), – can readily be personalised and adapted. The wording can, of course, be changed from "he" to "I" or "she", etc. When composing this prayer I was thinking more about 'feelings' than about the physical symptoms….

God our Father,
   when **Ian** feels diminished in illness,
   remind him that you call him by name   *Is 43:1*
   and hold him in the palm of your hand.

When he is worn out to nothingness,
   open his heart to the silence of longing for you.
Remind him that he must become as nothing
   so as to be filled with the fullness of your love.
When he feels fragile and broken,
   mould him and heal him,
   that he may more closely resemble
   the image of Jesus, your Son and our Brother.

When he is reminded of different times in the past,
   let him grow in the faith
   that you love him today, as he is,
   in the reality of his life this day.

When **Ian** is feeling uncertain about the future,
   lead him to that perfect love
   which casts out all fear.   *1 Jn 4:18*

When situations remind him
   – not of what he can do,
   but of what he cannot do –
   remind him that "love never fails",   *1 Cor 13:8*
   and that, living in your love,
   he will bear your fruit in plenty.   *Jn 15:5,9*

Nicholas Hutchinson

55 PRAYING FOR INDIVIDUALS

Lord Jesus, we read in the gospel
   that you spoke individually to many people
   and said:
"Be cured";   *Lk 5:13*
"Get up and walk";   *Lk 5:24*
"What do you want me
   to do for you?";   *Mt 20:32*
"Of course I want to cure you:
   be healed";   *Mt 8:3*
"Let what you want
   be done for you";   *Mt 9:29*
"Receive your sight";   *Lk 18:42*
"Receive back your hearing";   *Mk 7:34*
"Young man, arise";   *Lk 7:15*
"Go, your son will live";   *Jn 4:50*
"Go, your faith has saved you."   *Mk 10:52*

Knowing that you are present
   wherever your brothers and sisters are,
   and that you are keen to respond to our needs,
   I ask you today, Lord,
   to touch individually
   those people with special needs
   whom I have in mind.
I ask you to bring your healing touch to each of us
   in the way that is best for each individual.
Amen.

Nicholas Hutchinson

56 YOU COME TO MEET ME IN MY 'HERE AND NOW'

The days go on, Loving Lord,
   and, with increasing dosages of morphine,
   I grow more tired and 'out of things'
   in many ways.

As for my prayer, good Lord,
   I know that you do not need words.
My resting in your presence
   continues to be life-giving for me
   and I feel that, in order to pray,
   I would benefit from returning to a time
   when I had infinitely more energy
   and far greater 'wellness'.
Yet I know
   that my meeting with you is always NOW,
   and my prayer is NOW.
There is no need, as Isaiah reminds us,
   to keep looking to the past.
Instead it is always HERE AND NOW
   that I encounter you,
   and it is good that it is so.
You love me and you speak to me
   in this moment.
Your gift of yourself to me
   is here in the sacrament of the present moment:
   because it is always 'here and now'
   that you meet me, Lord.
I come before you, Lord, just as I am
   or, rather,
   you are already with me
   and know already how I am this day.
See my raised hand
   and accept it as a sign
   of my offering myself to you
   this day.

Nicholas Hutchinson, FSC

57 PRAYING FOR THOSE WHO DON'T EXPRESS CONCERN

I thank you, Father,
  for the many
  whose love and kindness
  and care and encouragement
  have been tangible.
They have been a great blessing for me.

I pray, too, for those
  who portray neither care nor interest,
  for whatever reasons,
  and I ask, Father, that I may be generous
  in the interpretations
  I put on their actions.

Nicholas Hutchinson

EIGHT

Affirmation: strengthening for the journey

58 PROGNOSIS

We all wonder how long we will live.
Some yearn for a long life,
others for an early demise.

We wonder how life will end.
Will it be long, drawn-out?
Or will it be sudden?

We wonder how we will cope with illness.
Will we be pain-free
or will we suffer?

Will we cope with death?
Will it overtake us reluctantly.
or will we reach out for it?

Do we view death as the end?
Do we view it as a new beginning,
Or are we indifferent to the future?

Some are given a prediction:
a prognosis of time left.
How do we use that time?

Is it used for tidying up our lives?
For getting affairs in order?
Or frittered on fretting?

Do we use that precious time positively
or is it full of regrets
for things not done?

continues...

Do we use the time to say those words
we need to say,
of love, forgiveness and comfort?

Do we leave behind good memories?
Do we make our loved ones know
how much they mean to us?

And do we help them afterwards to let go?
To recall the happy times,
release the negatives and move on?

Do we leave a legacy of warmth and joy,
of positive thoughts and hope?
– leaving the Earth a better place for our presence.
I hope so.

Barbara Harrison

59 MILESTONES AND MARKERS

There, Lord, was another milestone, another marker!
The prognosis had been "two years"
  remaining for me.
My second of the two expected birthdays passed
  and it was poignant to have had an 'extra' Christmas
  which I had not been expecting.
My approach had always been positive,
  looking to draw the good (and the humour!)
  out of all that happened to me.
That 'extra' Christmas was very beautiful for me
  and I enjoyed it in every respect.
Shortly afterwards came the celebration
  of New Year's Eve.
Fireworks seemed much louder and more brilliant
  than ever before,
  and I could hear people rejoicing
  at house parties and in local pubs.
It may have been the sense of fun being expressed
  but something special touched me that midnight.

I have experienced milestones before
  – such as deciding to go out by myself
  for one last drive in the car.
Then I returned, content and happy
  that I had made up my own mind
  much in advance
  of anyone thinking I would be 'unsafe' to drive.
Subtle as the difference may have been,
  I had transformed it into something positive
  because I had been the one
  to have made the decision.

And then there was the haircut.
A week before driving there
  I decided that that would be the last time
  that I would go under my own steam:
  it would be the last time
  as my own effort.   *continues...*

67

In future I would be dependent on others
    giving me a lift to this place or that.
People have always been very kind
    in asking if I would like to go anywhere,
    and I don't want to sound negative
    in saying that it's not the same
    as having my full choice and sense of control.

Hindsight can be a great teacher
    and, whilst I acknowledge how daft I can be,
    it is also the case
    that my judgement becomes impaired,
    as when I walked further than I should
    to get a taxi,
    when I should simply have phoned home.
Not only did the incident make me more ill,
    it alarmed some of those who love me.

I remember the occasion when I realised
    that I would no longer be able to go shopping
    even with the kindness of a driver
    parking right outside,
    and then accompanying me around the shop.
Yes, matters had moved on considerably,
    and my success
    in slowly walking around the house
    disguised the fact that greater distances,
    as well as the pressure of many people around me,
    had become tasks beyond me.

Yes, it was good to aim, to strive,
    but the horizons of my limitations
    were becoming much diminished.
The circumference of friends remained wide
    and I remained very touched
    by the kindness of those who visited me
    – even travelling many miles
    to do so.

Milestones have also been marked
  by the goodness of others
  who phone and write and email,
  and I am very touched
  by the generosity of so many people.

These, Lord, have been some of the 'milestones'
  or 'special markings'
  in recent times,
  recording significant happenings.

Remembering some very steep valley B-roads
  outside Oldham
  that carry signs that do not read 'Bend' or 'Care'
  but urge instead a 'reality-check'
  in stating *'Think'*,
  so it has been
  that certain experiences have brought me up sharp
  to see just how matters have been moving on.

I ask you to be with me, Lord,
  as I move on,
  as I slow down,
  as symptoms of one kind or another increase,
  as time needed in bed increases
  and as pain medication
  needs to be 'upped' further still.
Be with me, Lord,
  or – rather – help me to realise
  that you are already with me:
  you, Lord Jesus,
  who are my Way, my Truth and my Life. Amen.

Nicholas Hutchinson

60 LIVING LONGER THAN THE PROGNOSIS

Barbara Harrison (to her cousin, who had gone beyond his 2-year prognosis)

They said you had two years.
They have come and gone.
Your illness may have progressed,
But still you are here.

There has to be a reason.
A reason not known to us.
Your presence must be needed,
A mission to complete.

Not for us to question
Why suffering goes on.
We must just accept, then,
That there are still tasks to do.

It may be words stored in your heart,
It may be things you have to say,
It may be guidance or advice
Needed from your life.

It may be words unwritten,
It may be contacts new,
It may be friends remembered,
Or who remember you.

It may be revelations,
Not yet put into words
Or memories unshared yet,
Or prayers not prayed yet.

It may not be the time is right
It may not be the place,
It may be you are not ready
To shake off mortal coils.

Be sure that when the time is nigh,
More ready you will be,
But while you wait, make use of time
To ensure your task is done.

Barbara Harrison 12/12/2007

61   TOUCHED AND EMPOWERED BY GOD

Over my bed
   hangs a copy of Michelangelo's *Creation of Man*,
   showing the close-up of the hand of God
   giving life to Humanity.
God's finger is outstretched
   not only to humanity as a whole
   but offers life and love to me,
   to this individual,
   and each time I look at the painting
   whilst sitting at my desk
   and glancing at the wall above my bed,
   it touches and inspires me greatly
   – just as Michelangelo's brilliant artwork
   has inspired so many others,
   including cardinals
   who have assembled below the original artwork,
   to elect a new pope,
   there in the Sistine Chapel.

I think, Father,
   that this small section of the ceiling
   surely reflects a great personal touch:
   indicating the intimate, special relationship
   to which you call each of us,
   to which you invite each of us.

You call me, Father,
   to be faithful in that relationship:
   faithful to you as my Father and as my Friend.

St Augustine declared
   that anyone can, at any time,
   become a *'friend of God'*.
And, of course,
   that phrase is used in the scriptures:
Abraham is referred to   *Is 41:8*
   as 'the friend of God'.   *Jms 2:23*

continues...

There is much to think about
in the words of St John Chrysostom:
that *"there is nothing so good
as being the intimate friend of God".*

May I appreciate more and more
that it is to friendship with you,
Almighty God,
that you are calling me,
that you are inviting me. Amen.

Nicholas Hutchinson

*http://en.wikipedia.org/wiki/Sistine_Chapel_ceiling
www.vatican.vo/various/capelle/sistina_vr/index.html*

62   WALKING WITH THE LORD

Along the ordinary paths of my life, Lord,
you accompany me,
sharing my joys and my sorrows,
my hopes and my fears.

It is to you
who have already been before me
that I turn:
you who say
that the burden for those who follow you
is light.

In your strength, Lord,
and with you at my side,
I shall walk where you wish me to walk.
And when I fall,
I know that it will be you
who will bend low and reassure me
and lift my cross onto your shoulders.

Empower me with your Spirit and bless me,
and re-awaken in me each day
the joy and enthusiasm that arise
from knowing deep in my heart
that you are my Way, my Truth and my Life.

Renew in me each day, too,
the sense of being thankful always
for the many blessings in my life. Amen.

Nicholas Hutchinson

63 I NEED MY LOVED ONES TO 'LET ME GO'

For all my loved ones, Father,
for all special people in my life,
I want to express thanks at this time.
I think of faces and I think of names;
I smile and ask your blessing, Father,
– on all who have been accompanying me
as I have been preparing to die.

I appreciate my loves ones so very much
– especially as I grow ever closer to dying –
and I need them to express their love
in a particular way at this time.
What I mean is this, Father:
I need my loved ones to appreciate
that, although they and I
are about to go our different ways,
it is to a very special place
that Jesus is calling me.

continues...

There I hope to meet
  many other relatives and friends from the past,
  and it is there
  where I hope to meet many of *today's* loved ones
  when their own times come.

And there is something else I need
  from my loved ones here, Father,
  as I approach death.
**I need my loved ones to love me enough
  to 'let me go'.**
I need them to be 'comfortable' enough
  with the fact that I am dying.
I need to know
  that they are ready for me to depart,
  giving me the 'freedom' to leave **this** life
  so as to go in peace
  to the joyful and pain-free **new life**
  of love and happiness, of creativity and beauty
  that awaits me in Christ.
It's not, of course,
  that I am wanting them to convey the impression
  that they are eager for me to die!
My prayer is
  that nature takes its course rather speedily,
  and then, at the right time,
  Jesus will be there, Father,
  waiting to greet me and welcome me
  and bring me to you.

When some people are approaching death,
  some loved ones even pretend
  that the sick person will not die
  but will soon recover!
What's that all about?!
Denying reality can even be an insult
  to the intelligence of the sick person!

It might even be for me
   that I will only be able to be fully 'comfortable'
   in 'letting go' myself
   once I know that my loved ones
   are coming to terms with my departing.
They need to know, Father,
   that attempts to keep holding on to me,
   might prevent me from feeling really free
   in going to the next life – the fuller life –
   where I hope to meet them again in the future,
   just as I hope to meet others there
   who have died before me.
But die I must
   – and I am likely to struggle with dying
   if I think that my loved ones are so reluctant
   for me to depart.
They need to be reconciled with all of that,
   to be 'at one',
   with my being called to die at this time.

Whether there is pain for me or not, Father,
   my loved ones also need to know
   that I am very weary and drawn.
Everything in me
   is pointing towards the time fast-approaching
   when I **need** to die,
   and **when I die, it is not the end for me**
   – and it is essential that I proclaim that belief.
My earnest desire
   is to go to the life that Jesus has promised.
I only have one 'go' at dying (!)
   and whether death takes place during my sleep
   or whilst awake,
   I would like it to be a very special, blessed time,
   characterised (I do hope!)
   by everything being peaceful and gentle,
   with love
   and a warm sense of the Presence of God.

continues...

It is in heaven where I hope to join others
    who have died in faith,
    and it is where I hope
    that other loved ones will join me
    when their own times come in the future.

My relatives and friends need to know
    that I love them greatly
    and that I appreciate them joining me in praying
    for what is best for me
    – and my prayer
    is that I die sooner rather than later.
It is important, Father,
    that people realise
    that there is nothing morbid or negative
    in what I am saying.
Rather, I have tried, as always,
    to look at things through the eyes of faith.

Great as is my love, Father,
    for the special people in my life,
    (and great as is theirs for me)
    that love will continue after death.
I ask that my loved ones realise
    that, from the moment of my death,
    I will be praying for them.

I am grateful, Father,
    that Jesus proclaimed "blessed" those who mourn
    – because only those who love greatly can mourn.
I am very grateful that many are so blessed
    and I am very grateful
    that many have been so loving.

Nicholas Hutchinson

64 GOD IS FAITHFUL

I am pleased that there are glimpses from time to time of people and incidents from my past seeming to 'come together' and make something of a circle around me as I move forward: a circle whose focus is not myself. I can see that the centre instead is God and his commitment and faithfulness, rather than mine. As the length of days ahead of me decreases, I pray that the warmth of faith and of the presence of God will increase.

Lord, you look on us with love
  and call us to do the same
  to those to whom you send us.
Give us your vision
  and show us how to bring
  your blessings to others
  through our gaze and our presence.
Lead us to confirm for each person
  that you look on us with great love.
Bless us, Lord, this day and always. Amen.

Nicholas Hutchinson

65 MANY PEOPLE HAVE TOUCHED MY HEART

I am immensely grateful for so much, Lord,
  and particularly for many good people
  of all ages and backgrounds
  who, each in their own way,
  have contributed over the years
  to help make me the person that I am today.
Especially I ask for your blessing, Lord,
  on all who have been helping me
  on my journey in recent times,   *3 Jn 1:6*
  contributing so much love and concern,
  care and compassion.
Most particularly I think of my family,
  and I pray for them;
  their dear faces are so often before me.

continues...

Being seriously ill
  and with it taking me so long
  to do even simple things,
  I appreciate very much, Lord,
  that people have stepped in
  and, quietly and with no fuss,
  have been helping out:
  the laundry washed and a room cleaned,
  little jobs and the shopping done,
  bills sorted and a meal cooked.
I have valued a listening ear
  and gentle words between good friends,
  and I am grateful to so many people
  for standing by me
  and for supporting me (and those closest to me)
  during these times.

Nicholas Hutchinson

66 "FEELING VERY UNWELL"

As to how I am, Lord, it's difficult to describe...
It's not simply nausea or being sick from time to time.
Nor is it just being drawn and drained, with little energy
  (which contrasts with the good healthy tiredness
  that results from physical work).
Ordinary things in daily life do drain me
  not only of energy
  but also of the little 'wellness' and creativity
  that I still have from time to time.
I often thought it would be so good
  to 'slow down' a busy life,
  but slowing down in this way
  is not to be recommended!
I often experience difficulty

tolerating the smell of many foods,
and tastes have been changing,
 and there are eating and digestive
 and other problems,
I have experienced significant pain in the past
 but I am more than glad that pain is addressed now
 by a strong dosage
 of slow-release and other painkillers,
 although they contribute their own side-effects.
I have met people
 who experience pain breaking through each day,
 as well as others who have no pain.

As time goes on, Lord,
 I am conscious of more things happening in my body.
There are nights
 when sleep is shallow and short and broken,
 and there are days
 when deep sleep has lasted many hours,
 though it is never refreshing in the slightest,
 and other days see me slipping
 into unexpected periods of sleep at all times.
There are occasions when people comment
 that I look 'washed out' and 'worn out',
 even after a lengthy sleep!

Mainly, though, with this all-consuming illness,
 it is a matter of feeling so terribly ill
 in every cell of my body:
 feeling really 'horrible'.
Exactly how I am is very difficult to describe,
 and that itself is frustrating,
 as is the loss of concentration,
 such that I often need to rehearse people's names
 before they come into my room.
I know that you are with me.

Nicholas Hutchinson

67 MAKING DECISIONS, LETTING GO AND BEING READY TO 'MOVE ON'

After your Resurrection, good Lord,
  you said to Peter   *Jn 21:18*
  that, when young,
  he walked wherever he wished
  but, later in life, he would be bound
  and taken where he would rather not go.
And, just as Peter began to realise,
  I acknowledge, too, Lord,
  that I am not 'in control'
  of all that is happening to me
  – but I am learning to trust more, Lord,
  in your Providence, in your loving care,
  even amidst bad things
  that do happen to good people.

I seek not to let circumstances dictate decisions to me
  and, when I can, I try to pre-empt situations.

'Fighting' the illness is hard
  and I'm not sure it's productive.
I don't want to 'give in'
  if that means 'turning my face to the wall'
  in the sense of no longer looking
  to what is life-giving around me
  and no longer being life-promoting myself.
I do want to 'give in', though,
  in terms of 'letting go':
  adjusting more and more to 'letting go'.

What works for me in how I 'manage' the illness
  is to aim to 'go along' with the cancer,
  to 'ride' the condition:
  'surfing' its symptoms and its consequences.

I want to be free of unrelenting demands
  of so much sickness, exhaustion and debilitation.
You know, Lord, that I am so weary of it all!

Nicholas Hutchinson

68 MY FAMILY

You know my deep concerns, Lord,
   not only about being so profoundly ill
   but especially in anticipating
   the heart-wrenching event
   of leaving my family behind.
I know just how much I will miss them
   – and they me –
   and it's a particular concern for me
   as a loving wife and mother
   as to how my family will be
   when I am no longer around:
   how they will manage without me.
None of us is indispensable, of course,
   but I know only too well
   how I have supported others in the past,
   and how, in wanting to be supportive,
   I led the family to think
   that I would always be there for them
   (as I thought I would be!).
In good times and bad
   they have put their faith in me,
   trusting me and confiding in me.
My husband and my children
   are, in fact, my best friends.

In the past,
   when family members have faced difficulties
   of one kind or another,
   haven't I been the one that others could rely on,
   depend upon,
   who would always be there,
   who would pick up the pieces,
   be strong for others
   and help everyone to move on?

continues...

It's understandable, though, that I'm holding back
    at the thought of leaving my family behind.
The instinct of a wife and mother
    is so very strong.
How will my family adjust to my not being present
    with them and for them?
Part of me feels that I'm 'letting them down',
    although another part of me knows
    that that's a ridiculous thing to say.

On the one hand
    I would like my end to come quickly, Lord,
    but, on the other, sometimes I think
    – for family reasons –
    that I would like the end to be delayed,
    although that would take place
    only at a greater cost to me: taking more out of me.

I hope that my family want
    what is truly best for *me* and for *my* future
    but it's difficult for me because, in the past,
    whenever certain decisions have had to be made,
    I have always put my family before myself.
Is that not what a mother does?!
Help me, Lord, to be generous in a different way now:
    being generous to myself in thinking about *me*
    (as, indeed, I hope, my loved ones wish it to be)
    especially as regards
    the possibilities of further treatment or surgery
    needs to be balanced with 'quality of life'.
'Being alive' is not necessarily the same as 'living',
    and it means so much to me
    that my loved ones should be prepared to realise
    that extending my life
    is not necessarily the best thing.
Be with us all, Lord, in these difficult times.

Nicholas Hutchinson

69 MEDICAL PRACTITIONERS

I think of medical people and carers
   who have shared their skills and experience
   and have shown much care for me,
   and I am most grateful to them, Lord.
I can think of particular instances
   when much help and support and encouragement
   have been given
   – often through the simplest
   attitudes, actions and words –
   maybe of a nurse or a cleaner
   who says just the right words at just the right time.
I must add, though,
   that I have encountered some other medical people
   who have been lacking utterly
   in empathy and compassion
   and, evidently, in any real desire
   to reach out to others and seek to understand.
Their behaviour at the weakest time of my life
   did cause me to be disillusioned,
   amongst other things,
   but I pray for them, too.

Nicholas Hutchinson

70 'ANSWERS' AND GLIMPSES AND LEARNING FROM WHAT HAPPENS

I don't have 'answers', Lord,
  to the questions that many people have
  regarding suffering
  but, just occasionally I do get 'insights',
  'glimpses' of deeper things.
I do know for certain that there's no point
  in thinking *"If only..."* or *"What if..."*.
I can't turn the clock back and alter anything.
I know, too, that there's no point
  in thinking about laying 'blame' at anyone's door
  – nor does it serve any use
  to 'blame' *myself* in any way
  for this and that.
Instead, associating myself with Terry Waite,
  held for five years as a hostage in the Lebanon,
  I identify with the three resolutions he made:
  "No regrets,
  no sentimentality,
  and no self-pity."

I acknowledge that no devastating illness
  need diminish the person that I am
  nor detract from the unique vocation
  to which I am called **now, today,**
  because it is always **TODAY,** good Lord,
  that you tell Zacchaeus
  that you are entering
  his house, his home: *Lk 19:1-10*
  you are joining him in his 'special place'.
In *my* 'special place',
  in the home where *'I am who I am'*,
  in the home, Lord, where you choose to abide,
  is chronic illness which is terminal for me.
I know how important it is
  to accept that matters are as they are,
  and then move forward from there.
I rejoice that I live in a spirit of faith
  and that I have confidence in your love.

Each of us is called
　to bring loving kindness and compassion
　to every encounter and situation:
　seeking to help carry burdens
　and take upon ourselves
　some of the pain that others experience.

71　COMPASSION NEEDS TO BE MADE MANIFEST

Much is conveyed about compassion in this passage by Jean Vanier, from his book, Compassion DLT:

If compassion is to be a presence,
　it has to be made manifest by delicate signs:
　a letter, a phone call, an understanding look,
　a discreet gift which says:
　'I am with you; I carry it all with you.'
Compassion is a hidden
　and discreet communication
　which offers hope.
The distressed person is in danger
　of wallowing in despair and in the taste of death.
The compassionate friend is there
　to help another continue on the road,
　to live this time of mourning or distress
　with a tiny flame of hope....
Compassion is a word full of meaning.
It means: sharing the same passion,
　sharing the same suffering,
　sharing the same agony.
Accepting into my heart the misery in yours.
Your pain calls out to me; it touches my heart.
It awakens something within me,
　and I become one with you in your pain.
I may not be able to relieve your pain,
　but by understanding it and sharing it
　I make it possible for you to bear it
　in a way that enhances your dignity
　and helps you to grow.

72 PRAYING ALONGSIDE PEOPLE WHO ARE SUFFERING:

– reflecting with Job from the Old Testament.

This prayer, addressed to God the Father, incorporates some texts and themes from the Old Testament Book of Job (pronounced to rhyme with the word 'probe'). The person offering this prayer places self alongside others who are suffering, including Job and people suffering today, gaining strength especially from identifying with the suffering of Jesus.

Our choices about how to live can affect the lives of others.

Since becoming ill, Father,
   you know that I've tried my best
   to remain faithful to you,
   and I have offered as prayer to you
   my pain and suffering,
   my disorientation and diminished ability
   to do many things
   – asking that all of that be transformed
   into something good
   for the benefit of others.

Hoping that negative things can be 'transformed'
   into something that can be positive for others
   has helped in 'making some sense'
   of all that has been happening to me.

Father,
   my faith isn't strong enough to move mountains
   but I join my little faith
   to that of countless others,
   and I pray from the strength
   of knowing deep in my heart
   that *'you endowed me with life,*
   and watch each breath of mine
   with tender care.'

Job 10:12

Today I place myself
  alongside all those
  who need strength and healing:
  those who are sick,
  those who are tortured and in pain,
  those who suffer trauma of various kinds.

On the cross, Father,
  Jesus recited the opening words of a psalm,
  "My God, my God,
  why have you forsaken me?"   *Ps (21) 22:2*
  and I pray for others today
  who carry terrible crosses,
  whose experience is of feeling forsaken.

Whilst Jesus was identifying himself
  with those deep feelings of the psalmist,
  Jesus also knew
  that most of those in earshot
  would have recognised the psalm
  and would think, too,
  of its positive ending in hope,
  which declares your faithfulness, Father,
  to the people you call your own.
In certain moments, Father,
  maybe I can identify
  both with despair and with hope,
  and there are times when my feelings
  are more negative than positive.
I ask for strength in bearing the difficult cross
  that I am carrying:
  a cross for which I have felt each blow of the nails
  as I was affixed to it, and it to me.
But then, of course,
  if it was extremely light to carry,
  it wouldn't really be a cross, would it?

Diminished and overwhelmed as I am at times
  with this illness and its many consequences,
  I feel like Job in the Old Testament
  whose world fell apart,
  and who lost so much that was dear to him.

continues...

I pray for those like Job
who wonder at night:
"When will it be day?"
and in the daytime think,
"How slowly evening comes!"   *Job 7:4*
I am conscious
that those can be some symptoms
of people who experience the pit of depression,
and as I pray now
I place myself alongside those who are depressed
and alongside those
who feel very low or disorientated at times.

I bring before you, Father,
those who have *'fear come over them,*
at the thought of all they suffer.'   *Job 9:28*
I pray for those
who have *'terrors turn to meet them,'*
for those whose *'confidence is blown away*
as if by the wind,'
for those whose *'life trickles away,*
as they are gripped by days of grief."
At night-time there are those
for whom sickness can sap their bones
and they can feel gnawed
by wounds that never sleep.   *Job 30:15-18*

You grew angry, Father,
– not with Job, who had suffered much
but with his so-called 'comforters', his 'friends',
who did not speak honestly and from the heart
(unlike Job
in his understandable desolation and despair).

For some people,
the great losses equivalent to those of Job
might be of the death of a loved one,
or a relationship broken down;
for others it might be the loss of health
or of employment or their home.

In all such circumstances
　　it is good and strengthening
　　to be consoled by true friends,
　　to be truly comforted.
Yet 'Job's comforters'
　　– the term has even entered our language –
　　'Job's comforters' were false,
　　professing to comfort him
　　whilst in reality doing the very opposite,
　　trying to persuade him to give up and curse God.

In the end, Father,
　　we read that you restored Job's fortunes
　　because he had prayed for his friends   *Job 42:10*
　　and he trusted in you.
I am not looking, Father,
　　for any kind of 'restoration of fortunes':
　　such seeking would be to reduce matters to 'magic'
　　and would 'trivialise'
　　what your loving care is all about:
　　your love
　　from which nothing can separate us: *Rom 8*
　　your love over which nothing can triumph.

On that hill of Gethsemane,
　　utter evil
　　confronted the fullness of God's goodness.
As I now picture myself, Father,
　　in the presence of Jesus
　　whilst he underwent the agonies of breathing,
　　minute by minute,
　　on the cross,
　　I can reflect on a few occasions
　　when I have perceived utter evil
　　seeking to have its day
　　(sometimes of evil 'slipping in'
　　between otherwise good people
　　when some have lost direction in their lives).

continues...

And so, Father,
    it is with the conviction
    of the lived experience of your love,
    that I can join your beloved Son, my Brother,
    saying – as he did –
    "Into your hands, Father,
    I commend my spirit",   *Lk 23:46; Ps (30) 31:6*
    I am saying, Father,
    that I give you my whole self,
    and I ask you to look after, too,
    all those people I now have in mind:
    all who are in torment of one kind or another.

Words often are not easy, Father,
    especially when difficulties come close
    to overwhelming people.
Instead of my words,
    take the deepest longings of my heart
    and hear the words of Jesus, your Son,
    who calls us his friends   *Lk 8:21*
    and wishes his peace and joy upon us.   *Jn 15:14*

This prayer for those in torment
    I make, Father,
    in the confidence of Jesus, our brother,
    who said that you love us
    as you love him. Amen.

Nicholas Hutchinson

73 JESUS ACCOMPANIES US, MAKES HIS HOME IN US, AND CHOOSES TO SUFFER WITH US

I know of your uniqueness, Lord Jesus,
   in being truly God and truly a human being.
Your becoming human
   has made the humanity of all of us very special,
   and I am called and invited
   to learn from you
   the way to live fully as a human being.

It gives me strength in realising
   that both you and I, Lord,
   have experienced suffering:
   each in our own ways.
And your presence in my suffering now, Lord,
   helps me to transform it,
   helping me to grow as the person you call me to be.

Through prayer
   – through my talking with you as a friend –
   I become more and more aware
   that, with your hand upon my shoulder,
   you accompany me each day and share my joy:
   but you are committed also
   to share my pain, discomfort and suffering.
That makes a great difference to me, Lord,
   as it does to appreciate
   that, amidst what is happening to me,
   'there is no spot
   where you are not'.
You are with me, Lord,   *Ps 139*
   above me and below me,   *& St Patrick's Breastplate*
   to my left and to my right,
   ahead of me in what is to come,
   and behind me
   in healing relationships
   and redeeming happenings from my past.
There is nothing, Lord Jesus,
   that can ever separate me   *Rom 8:35*
   from you and your love.

continues...

Friends support each other,
  are happy with each other,
  smile and laugh together
  and, in really feeling for each other,
  there are times
  when friends also cry with each other.
We read in the Gospel, for instance,
  that you wept   *Jn 11:35*
  when your friend Lazarus died.
Yes, Lord, you wept,
  and the people said: *"See how much he loved him"*
– so strong was your love for Lazarus.

'Tears of God' is the translation,
  of *'Deora De'*, the Irish Gaelic name
  for the beautiful plant that is also called 'fuchsia'.
And now, when I see fuchsia, Lord,
  I am reminded
  of your whole-hearted commitment to me,
  to the extent of your shedding tears of love with me
– as loved ones do at times with each other.

Nicholas Hutchinson

74 TO YOUR KINGDOM

Through your Incarnation, Lord Jesus,
  – your becoming a human being –
  and through your Resurrection from the dead,
  we can discover that the meaning of life
  is to be found in love.
My faith is strong
  in the better and fuller life that comes after this,
  where I will be greeted again by many loved ones:
  by those who went ahead of me some time ago.

Even though I have cherished so much
  in this present life,
  I join those who proclaim:
'If we die with you,
  then we shall live with you.   *2 Tim 2:11-13*
If we hold firm, then we shall reign with you.
You are always faithful."

And when I arrive in your Kingdom, Lord,
  I will remember before you many loved ones,
  and when they themselves breathe their last
  and arrive before you, Lord,
  I will be there to greet them
  and will welcome them warmly.

                    Nicholas Hutchinson

75 BEING POSITIVE OR NEGATIVE, AND BEING REALISTIC

I am grateful, Lord, that some people
  have been able to step into my shoes
  and really begin to 'feel' something
  of what all of this is like for me.
I have appreciated it very much
  when people have indicated in all sorts of ways
  that they have wanted to try to understand.
Even if they don't understand fully,
  it is their *trying* to understand
  which makes all the difference to me.

A good 'test' to indicate
  whether or not someone is, indeed, really committed
  to trying to understand the one who is very ill,
  is whether or not
  they do communicate to the sick person
  the good wishes that an individual has requested
  be passed on.
Another such 'test'
  is to see if others give 'openers'
  for the sick person to talk about
  what he or she wishes,
  including openness
  to talk about illness and its consequences,
  and without the other person
  changing the topic of conversation.

One of the most *difficult* things for me, Lord,
  is when a few people confuse my being realistic
  – my seeing it all as it really is –
  with what they call being *'negative'*!
Their misunderstanding
  flies in the face of my being known
  as a cheerful, life-giving,
  'glass-half-full' kind of person,
  who always looks on the bright side of things.

Essential as it is
  for the patient to accept how matters are,
  it undermines the person who is ill
  if loved ones do not do the same:
  if family and friends do not take on board
  the reality of the person's circumstances.
Their trying to persuade me that I will be well again
  (when it is abundantly evident that I will not!)
  seems to be an attempt
  to get me to live in a 'pretend' never-never world,
  which would be of help to no-one.
It can be upsetting and frustrating for me, Lord,
  though I aim not to show it,
  but it can mark something of a parting of our ways,
  especially if I sense
  that they tend to want to 'preserve' me, as if to say,
  rather than 'allow' me to depart.
It's as though they have wanted to walk beside me
  but only *so far*:
  only on condition
  that the road doesn't take a particular direction,
  which it certainly will!
I want my loved ones to join me fully,
  and that is my prayer:
  that they may accept
  the reality that is happening to me.

Nicholas Hutchinson

76 LEARNING FROM OTHERS AND GROWING

I remember meeting several cancer patients
  who had no-one to accompany them in any sense.
I pray, Lord, for them
  and for all those who are worse off than myself.

Throughout this time of terminal illness,
  when there has been so much to learn
  about living as a human being,
  I have been very touched
  at the way some people have made me feel
  about myself, about others, and about situations,
  and I am very grateful to them.
I hope, too,
  that there might be something life-promoting
  in the way that I and others are 'living with dying'
  which might be of some kind of help to someone
  in the future.

I pray for any loved ones
  who may not yet have joined me
  in understanding just how things are.
I know it is important
  that their eyes and minds and hearts
  be open to the reality of my circumstances,
  and I pray for those blessings for them.

Through everything, loving Lord,
– including pain and suffering
  and difficulties of various kinds –
  keep my eyes open
  to so much love and compassion,
  to so much beauty and creativity,
  and to so much that is wonderful
  within and around me.
Empower me with your Spirit
  so that I may remain very grateful, good Lord,
  for so much. Amen.

Nicholas Hutchinson, FSC

NINE
"Leading us home"

77 TO REALISE MORE AND MORE HOW I AM LOVED BY GOD

In an email at the start of the New Year, and with the
prognosis pointing to approximately a year's life remaining for me,
a good friend wrote these words of wisdom:

"Greetings and good wishes for a very happy New Year. I
hope that does not sound hollow in your circumstances.
I so wish that this will be the very best year of your life,
and that you will be filled with peace and joy –
that you will realise more and more how you are loved by God."

78 I SHALL SEE THE SHINING CITY

There will come a time, O Lord,
when my links with earth grow weaker,
when my powers fail;
when I must bid farewell to dear ones
still rooted in this life
with their tasks to fulfil
and their loved ones to care for;

when I must detach myself
from the loveliest things
and begin the long journey.
Then I shall hear the voice
of my beloved Christ, saying:
"It is I; be not afraid".

So, with my hands in his,
from seeming dark valley
I shall see the shining City
and climb with trusting steps,
and be met
by the Father of souls
and clasped in the everlasting arms.

George Appleton

79 GOD WAITS FOR ME TO RETURN HOME AND TELL MY STORY

I still believe deeply that our few years on this earth are part of a much
larger event that stretches out far beyond the boundaries of our birth
and death. I think of it as a mission into time: a mission that is very
exhilarating and even exciting, mostly because the One who sent me
on the mission is waiting for me to come home and tell the story of
what I have learned.

Henri Nouwen
'Life of the Beloved', New York, Crossroad, 1992

80 THE CLOWN'S PRAYER

As I stumble through this life,
help me to create more laughter than tears,
dispense more happiness than gloom,
spread more cheer than despair.

Never let me become so indifferent
that I will fail to see
the wonder in the eyes of a child
or the twinkle in the eyes of the aged.

Never let me forget
that my total effort
is to cheer people, make them happy,
and forget – at least momentarily –
all the unpleasantness in their lives.

And, in my final moment
may I hear you whisper:
*"When you made My people smile,
you made Me smile."*

(author unknown)

81 PEOPLE ARE 'GIFTS' WHOM I PRAY FOR BOTH BEFORE AND AFTER MY DEATH

Countless people over the years
   have touched my life in all sorts of ways,
   and a 'present' I can make to them
   arising from my relatively early death
   will consist of my praying for them with great love
   for the remainder of their lives.
Some I have known by name;
   others left an impact only momentarily,
   and their names, Father,
   are known only to you.

continues...

I believe that all of these, Father,
   were treasured individuals
   whom you wanted
   to have a part to play in my life
   (or me in theirs)
   however briefly.
They were people you 'gave me' specially
   (just as you gave me to others):
   the same kind of people
   whom Jesus prayed about with warmth,
   when he considered as 'gifts'   *Jn 17:9-12,24*
   the people you had given to him.

Nicholas Hutchinson

82 BECOMING A TRUER AND MORE FAITHFUL FRIEND

When I breathe my last, Father,
   may my eyes open again
   in the place where I will see you face-to-face
   and hear you welcome me by name.
May I be blessed in hearing you say
   that you are very fond of me:
   blessed, too, in realising
   that you do, indeed, call me your friend.
Amen.

Nicholas Hutchinson

TEN
Into your hands

83 YOU ARE CLOSE TO ME

Loving Father,
 I appreciate that you delight   *cf Mic 7:18*
 in every one of your beloved people.
I know that it was with great love
 that you crafted each of us
 from the dust of the earth.   *cf Gen 2:7*
We are the clay, Father; you are the potter, *Is 64:7*
 and all of us are the work of your hands.
Into our nostrils
 you breathed forth your Spirit,
 giving life to our flesh,
 summoning us to live
 in the light of your image and likeness. *Gen 1:26*

It is for me a wonder
 that until my last breath
 you will continue creating me
 as your work of art,   *Eph 2:10*
 and I know
 that "your fingers can touch nothing
 but to mould it into loveliness." *George MacDonald*

I ask forgiveness, Father,
 for times when I have
 tarnished the image and likeness
 and marred the integrity of the blueprint
 that you have had in mind
 whenever you have thought of me.
I ask forgiveness, too, Father,
 for times when I have walked in darkness, *cf Is 9:1*
 failing to match
 the glory, the brilliance, the transfiguration *Lk 9:28-36*
 that you have had in mind for me
 in proclaiming 'good'
 everything that you have made. *Gen 1:31*

continues...

In our world that you love so much, Father, *Jn 3:16*
  I thank you for restoring our dignity
in Jesus, your Word made flesh, *Jn 1:14*
  whose image you see
  whenever you look at us.
He is Risen and accompanies us now, *Lk 24*
  and my heartfelt prayer
  is to know Jesus
  and the power of his Resurrection, *Phil 3:10*
  and to have the love of Christ overwhelm me. *2 Cor 5:14*
Jesus invites me to be 'fully alive' *St Irenaeus*
  in a world 'charged with the grandeur of God', *G.M.Hopkins*
  if only I open my eyes to see *cf Jn 9:32*
  all that is around me.

As children look like their parents,
  may others recognise us, Father,
  as bearing your looks and characteristics.
I ask, Father, that we may grow more like you,
  grateful that it is in you
  that we live and move and have our being. *Acts 17:28*
In the time remaining to each of us, then,
  we need your help, Father,
  to live out your own qualities
  which we have inherited from you,
  and we need to be enabled by your Spirit
  to live out the shared vision, for example, *cf Prov 29:18*
  of being kind and full of compassion, *Ps 145:8*
  of healing the broken-hearted,
  of binding up all their wounds, *cf Ps 147:3*
  of being good and honourable, *Phil 4:8*
  and of being so cheerful
  that it overflows to others. *2 Cor 5:18*

In the time left to me, Father,
  I pray that I may remain
  in the peace and serenity
    that you have given me so far,
  in the faith
    on which you have helped me build my life,
  and in the growing awareness
    of your life-giving presence and loving Providence.

Nicholas Hutchinson

84 THANKS FOR MANY ENCOUNTERS

1. Soon I will be coming to you, Loving Father,
      and I reflect now
      on so many blessings
      you have given to me over the years.

2. I am conscious
      of so much beauty and so much delight
      that I have experienced,
      and I thank you
      that you have kept my eyes and ears open.
   I thank you that your Spirit
      has inspired me in many ways.

3. Soon, Father, I will be coming to you,
      and I am conscious
      of so much love and affection
      that has come my way,
      and I am most grateful, Father,
      for so many individuals
      who have been part of my life.

4. I rejoice in the many people
      who have accompanied me in so many ways
      over my lifetime,
      and most especially in the last few years.
   I ask you to return, Lord, many times over
      the warmth and love, the care and affection
      that I have been shown.
   I am grateful that all of that
      has been a reflection, too,
      of your own love and compassion for me
      and for us all.
   With confidence, Father,
      I place myself into your hands.

continues...

5. Soon, Father, I will be coming to you.
   I look forward to meeting again
   many people I have known and loved from the past.
   When the time is right,
   I look forward to them gathering to welcome me
   and then lead me forward to you.
   Amongst them will be some young people
   whose early part of their lives
   you enabled me to touch with your grace.

6. It will be good to smile and walk alongside each other
   as we journey together once again
   to life in all its richness and abundance
   in your presence.

7. Friends and relatives will be there, too,
   as well as others who have touched my life:
   many an individual
   whose life and death have influenced me,
   and they will accompany me still further.

8. And then it will be Jesus, your Son and my Brother,
   who will take my hand in his
   – his hand which bears the marks of love.
   And in that touch
   I know that I will sense in all its fullness
   what it is to be redeemed and healed
   and made whole.

9. Then, as Jesus leads me forward the next few steps,
   will he introduce me to you, Father,
   or will you smile and show me your hand
   where it will be clear to see
   that, there, my name is written?
   I look forward so much
   to all that it means to be clasped in your arms,
   enfolded in your life,
   and encompassed, embraced, in your love.

10. And then I will ask your blessing, Father,
    on so many who have enriched my life.
  There, too, I trust,
    will be those I know
    who have plumbed the depths of darkness,
    whose burdens
    have often come close to crushing them,
    and whose lives, I hope,
    I might have touched somehow with your love.
  I will ask you to bless them and make them whole,
    just as others have blessed me
    and have prayed
    that I might be made whole.

11. I will remember, too, Father,
    those I have wounded
    and those who have wounded me,
    that all of us may be embraced
    in your love and care, your mercy and kindness.
  With confidence, Father,
    I place myself into your hands.

Nicholas Hutchinson

85 LORD, REMEMBER ME

We ask the Lord Jesus
  to remember each of us,
  as we recall the Good Thief
  dying beside Jesus on the cross,
  who said to him:
"Lord, remember me
  when you come into your kingdom…"

Could SING 'Jesus, Remember me'
on the Taizé cassette/CD: Laudate
or on the Taizé CD Sing to God

86 LITANY OF MARY, AT THE HOUR OF OUR DEATH

(a prayer requesting the help of the Blessed Virgin Mary)

1. Mary, chosen by God,
   believing the angel's message,
   accepting the will of God:
   pray for us sinners
   now, and at the hour of our death.

2. Mary, the handmaid of the Lord,
   filled with the Holy Spirit;
   Mary, proclaiming:
   "let what you have said be done in me":
   pray for us sinners
   now, and at the hour of our death.

3. Mary, unmarried, yet conceiving
   trusting, whilst not knowing
   what others would say of you;
   Mary, ever lowly, giving glory to God;
   Mary, full of grace:
   pray for us sinners
   now, and at the hour of our death.

4. Mary, welcoming shepherds and wise men;
   Mary, Mother of Christ,
   rejoicing in God your Saviour:
   pray for us sinners
   now, and at the hour of our death.

5. Mary, blessed because you believed
   that the promise made you by the Lord
   would be fulfilled;
   Mary, ever faithful,
   hearing the word of God and keeping it:
   pray for us sinners
   now, and at the hour of our death.

6. Mary, beside Jesus at Cana;
   Mary, inspiring trust,
   saying: *"Do whatever he tells you";*
   Mary, faithful disciple of your Son:
   pray for us sinners
   now, and at the hour of our death.

7. Mary, whose love met Jesus
   as he carried his cross;
   Mary, whose love meets us as we carry our crosses;
   Mary, with Jesus in his agony:
   pray for us sinners
   now, and at the hour of our death.

8. Mary, waiting with the apostles at Pentecost;
   Mary, pilgrim in faith:
   pray for us sinners
   now, and at the hour of our death.

9. Mary, treasuring all these things
   and pondering them in her heart:
   pray for us sinners
   now, and at the hour of our death.

Nicholas Hutchinson

87 'HIGH FLIGHT'

A poem by
John Gillespie Magee (1922-41)

It was in 1941, during the darkest days of the Second World War, that John
Magee – a young Canadian pilot in the Royal Air Force – wrote this vivid poem
about the spirit and adventure of flying, and he writes of putting out his hand and
'touching the face of God'. Three months later, at the age of 19, he was killed in
an air collision. On his grave in the village of Scotwick in Lincolnshire are inscribed
the first and last lines of his poem:
'Oh! I have slipped the surly bonds of Earth,
Put out my hand and touched the face of God.'

Oh! I have slipped the surly bonds of Earth
And danced the skies on laughter-silvered wings;
Sunward I've climbed, and joined the tumbling mirth
Of sun-split clouds – and done a hundred things
You have not dreamed of
– wheeled and soared and swung
High in the sunlit silence. Hov'ring there,
I've chased the shouting wind along, and flung
My eager craft through footless halls of air.
Up, up the long, delirious burning blue
I've topped the wind-swept heights with easy grace,
Where never lark, or even eagle flew –
And, while with silent, lifting mind I've trod
The high untrespassed sanctity of space,
Put out my hand and touched the face of God.

http://en.wikipedia.org/wiki/John_Gillespie_Magee

www.prayingeachday.org/Jan28.pdf

(See '28 January' in the author's 3-volume book, 'Praying Each Day of the Year' –
ISBN 1 898366 30 6)

88 THE VEIL BETWEEN IS VERY THIN

John O'Donohue
'Anam Chara' (Bantam Books), pg 256

When a person is close to death,
the veil between this world and the eternal world
is very thin.

The following prayer was written shortly after learning that cancer was terminal.
The person praying gives thanks for much, and prays for those left behind. If the
author had not been celibate – involving not being married – such a prayer would,
of course, have reflected much on the leaving behind of a wife and family.

Living, dying and going home

Loving Father, faithful God,   *1 Cor 1:9*
   as I remember before you
   those who have died,
   I reflect, as well, upon the time remaining to me.
I ask you to touch my heart and renew my spirit,
   so that I may live in such a way
   that I express thanks every day
   for so many blessings.
And when I bid farewell to this world
   remember, Father, your own tender care of me.
Having guided me
   since I left my mother's womb   *Job 31:18*
   you have called me by name,   *Is 43:1*
   declared me precious in your eyes,   *Is 43:4*
   and watched each breath I have taken.   *Job 10:12*

And when I breathe my last,
   look not at my sin, Father,
   but at the face of Jesus,
   my Brother and Redeemer.
Hear him say that he called me his friend,   *Jn 15:15*
   made his home in me,   *Jn 15:4*
   and walked beside me
   through the valley of darkness.   *Ps 23:4*

continues...

Remember, too, Father, that your Holy Spirit
    has dwelt in me and prayed in me,   *Rom 8:11,26*
    and helped me in my weakness.
Listen to the Spirit speak on my behalf.   *cf Jn 14:26*

Enfold me then in your love, Father,
    as I know you embrace me now,
    and admit me, I pray,
    to your kingdom of light, happiness and peace,
    to the place that you have prepared for me,   *Mt 25:34*
    alongside those I love
    and beside many who have gone before me,
    marked with the sign of faith:
    there to see you face-to-face,   *1 Cor 13:12*
    where pain and suffering will be no more.

And when the earth encloses my body, Father,
    look then at the faith and compassion
    of those who have surrounded me
    with their love.
Bring them comfort, Father,
    since only those who love can mourn,
    and assure them
    that I will remember them before you   *cf Lk 23:42*
    in your kingdom. Amen.

(This prayer could be used at the graveside)

Nicholas Hutchinson

ELEVEN
Farewell and mourning

89 A PRAYER OF FAREWELL

Inspired by texts in Scripture, in the Liturgy, and in the Fathers of the Early Church

ALL

Go forth, N, upon your final journey.
Go from this world and rest in peace
  in the presence of God the Father,
  who created you;
  in the love of Jesus our Lord,
  who calls you his friend,
  and in the warmth of the Holy Spirit,
    who has made his home in you.

Reader 1

In death
  your life is changed, not ended,
  and we give you back to our faithful God
  who first gave you to us.
On our common pilgrimage
  we have accompanied you
  as far as we can go together.
Our ways part for now
  but, beyond our horizon,
    you will be met by Jesus
    who is himself the Way.

continues...

May the angels lead you into paradise,
  and the saints take you by the hand
  and walk with you into the presence of God.
There, face-to-face,
  you will meet our loving Father.
His hands will be swift to welcome,
  and he will hold you close:
  his tender love
  is that of a mother for her child,
  and he has written your name, N,
  on the palm of his hands.

Reader 2

You will find rest
  in Christ, the Good Shepherd,
  who carries you and says: "Do not be afraid."
His peace will be yours
  in a place where pain and sorrow
  will be no more.
There in God's kingdom
  of light, happiness and peace
  the Holy Spirit will heal and renew
  and strengthen you.
The end of your pilgrimage
  will be a new beginning
  in the bright dawn of eternal day.

ALL

Go forth, N, upon your final journey.
Go from this world, and be with God.

Nicholas Hutchinson

*(This Prayer of Farewell can be used in accompanying the dying, or be recited
by one or more family members or friends at the funeral. Paragraphs 1, 3 and 5
could be recited together by several people, if not for everyone to recite if the text
is printed in a booklet.)*

90 WE GIVE THEM BACK TO YOU, LORD

Thought to have been written by William Penn.

We give them back to you, O Lord,
　who first gave them to us;
　and as you did not lose them in the giving,
　so we do not lose them in the return.

Not as the world gives do you give,
　O lover of souls.
　For what is yours is ours also
　if we belong to you.

Life is unending because love is undying,
　and the boundaries of this life
　are but an horizon,
　and an horizon is but the limit of our vision.

Lift us up, strong Son of God,
　that we may see further.
Strengthen our faith
　that we may see beyond the horizon.

And while you prepare a place for us
　as you have promised,
　prepare us also for that happy place,
　that where you are, we may be also,
　with those we have loved, forever.

91 PRAYER IN THE GARDEN

Loving Father,
  like clay in the hands of the potter   *Sir 33:13*
  you have made each of us   *Jer 18:1-4*
  your magnificent work of art.   *Eph 2:10*
Open our eyes each day   *Jn 9*
  to appreciate the beauty
  that is within and around us,
  leading us home to you.

The path that Jesus chose to walk
  would lead him to the cross,
  and as we think of his agony
  in the Garden called Gethsemane,   *Mt 26:36-56*
  we pray for all at this time
  who are carrying the burden
  of sickness or loneliness,
  discouragement or sadness,
  and for all who support them.
As the sun rose on that first Easter Day
  the Risen Jesus walked in the garden
  where he had been lain.   *Jn 20:15*

At this, the end
  of our **brother's/sister's** journey,
  we ask you, Father,
  to call **his/her** name again
  and welcome **N** into your arms.
Embrace **him/her** in your healing love
  in that Garden which is Paradise.

We rejoice that the Risen Jesus
  walks beside us now   *cf Lk 24*
  and blesses us as we mourn *N/.*   *Mt 5:5; Lk 6:21*

Nicholas Hutchinson

92 'CLOSURE'

In the weeks and months ahead, good Lord,
   grant a deep peace
   to those who have lost loved ones.
Bring them some kind of 'closure'
   in the times ahead,
   that they may be strengthened
   to be of help to others
   whose experience has been similar.

Nicholas Hutchinson

93 ONLY THOSE WHO LOVE GREATLY CAN MOURN

Lord Jesus, you tell us
   that those who mourn are blessed,
   knowing that only those who love greatly
   can mourn.
We know, too,
   that it is better to have loved and lost someone
   than never to have loved at all.
May ***N's*** family
   find strength and peace
   through the support and kindness of others,
   knowing that other people care for them
   and hold them in prayer. Amen.

Nicholas Hutchinson

94 HEALING AND PEACE FOR THOSE WHO ARE MOURNING

Father,
    bring courage and strength
    to those who now mourn
    because they have loved greatly.
In your loving kindness
    bring them healing and inner peace,
    and lead the one they mourn
    into your kingdom
    of light, happiness and peace.

Nicholas Hutchinson

95 DYING; SHIP OVER THE HORIZON

Based on a passage by Victor Hugo from his 'Toilers of the Sea'

What is dying?
The ship sailed away
    and I stand watching till it fades on the horizon
    and someone at my side says:
    "The ship is gone."
Gone where? Gone from my sight, that is all;
    the ship is just as large as when I saw it.
As I see the ship grow smaller and go out of sight
    it is just at that very moment
    that there are others in a different place
    who say:
    "Watch; here the ship comes",
    and other voices take up a glad shout:
    "You have arrived"
    – and that is what dying is about.

Four poems follow from a series written by Barbara Harrison, whose husband John died in 2007 at a relatively young age, suffering from Lewy Body Dementia. Barbara was among those whose partner no longer recognised her – hence such phrases as "but the mourning began a long time ago" and "relief for his freedom". In her husband's death, Barbara writes of herself as being "one half of a whole, no longer complete". Mourning contributes to some kind of closure, and in the poem, 'Scattering the Ashes', it is very poignant to read that John's wife and son decided to avail of his hobby of flying gliders (having been an aircraft designer) to be the means of releasing his ashes: "Two planes together / Widow in one / (adult) Son in the other / Ashes released… / God bless / Soar peacefully."

JOHN'S END OF LIFE

Barbara Harrison

Ill for so long
It happened so fast
Its speed unexpected.

Hours only ailing,
Discomfort short-lasting
The end overwhelming

He knew we were there
Saw his son
Then knew he could go.

He left in a hurry
Hardly time for goodbye
And was gone.

His essence remains.
Memories are vivid.
The farewell is said

Bereavement begins
But the mourning began
A long time ago.

New routines needed.
Unwanted freedoms.
Desolate loss.

John has gone.

97 ALONE

I feel so alone now,
Now that he's gone.

The days are long now,
The nights are too,

The sun's less bright,
Clouds are greyer now,

Nothing is the same now,
Now he's gone.

Problems are more intense,
The solutions, less clear,

Crowds are more menacing,
Individuals, more daunting.

Identity is not certain,
Confidence, lacking.

One half of a whole.
No longer complete.

Adjustment is slow,
Getting used to his loss,

Adapting to new reality
Now that he's gone.

Barbara Harrison

98 THE FUNERAL

It had dreamlike quality,
Disbelief; not true,
Could he really have died?

Yet, here was the hearse,
The coffin and flowers.
What more proof did I need?

Funeral cars moving slowly,
Family members together,
Deep in thought.

To the chapel we followed,
Saw the casket unloaded.
Was that really him, there?

He led: us behind,
Those gathered; sympathetic,
Supportive and sad.

Service of closure,
Words of comfort and solace,
Music; emotive and apt.

Composure so fragile,
Tears very close.
But relief for his freedom.

Goodbye unavoidable,
Final gesture farewell,
Hopes and dreams ended.

Last sad reflections,
Life's curtain falls
And he's gone.

Barbara Harrison

99 SCATTERING THE ASHES

It was a beautiful day,
Blue, sunny skies
White filmy clouds
And a warm breeze.

Two gliders ready
Two pilots willing
To carry out his wishes
In flight.

Bumpy tug take-off,
Surging onwards
And upwards
Like birds.

Height reached,
Tug rope released,
Freedom to soar,
Dip and turn.

Clear visibility,
Scenery he knew,
Landmarks familiar,
Other gliders too.

Two planes together
Widow in one,
Son in the other;
Ashes released.

Floating downwards
Over the airstrip
Where he flew many times
One last pass of farewell.

God Bless.
Soar peacefully.

Barbara Harrison

100 A SAFE LODGING

May the Lord support us all the day long,
till the shades lengthen and the evening comes
and the busy world is hushed,
and the fever of life is over
and our work is done.
Then, in his mercy,
may he give us a safe lodging and a holy rest,
and peace at the last. Amen.

Blessed John Henry Newman

SOME PRAYER WEBSITES

1 Prayer website of Nicholas Hutchinson:
   www.prayingeachday.org

2 Prayer for the Day
   www.holyfamilybordeaux.org/prayer_for_the_day.asp

3 'Pray as you go' – scripture of the day, reflective text and music
   which can be downloaded for use via a computer or, if travelling,
   via an iPod
   www.pray-as-you-go.org

4 Receiving the day's scripture texts as an email
   www.dailygospel.org

5 Reflection on the day's scripture
   www.creighton.edu/CollaborativeMinistry/daily.html

6 'Sacred Space'
   www.sacredspace.ie

7 INTERCESSIONS
   a) Intercessions for each day of the year, corresponding with the
      Mass readings (Diocese of Adelaide)
      www.adelaide.catholic.org.au/daily-intercessions-for-mass

   b) St Louis University, USA – intercessions for Sunday Masses
      http://liturgy.slu.edu/

   c) RP Books – click on Free Bidding Prayers which, being posted
      on Friday afternoons, includes prayers regarding current
      news items
      www.rpbooks.co.uk

INDEX